This

NUCLEAR SPECIES

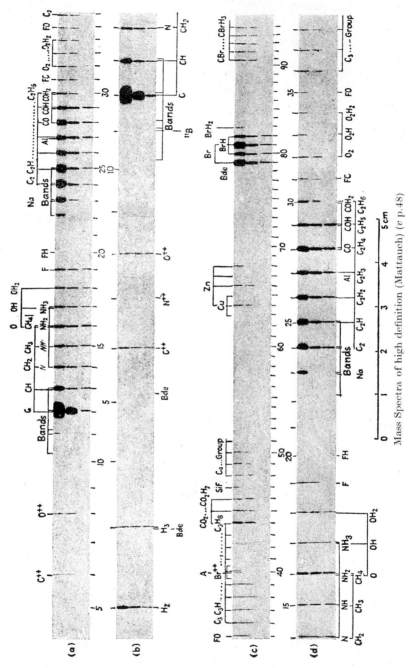

Mass Spectra of high definition (Mattauch) (v p. 48)

Frontispiece

NUCLEAR SPECIES

BY

H. E. HUNTLEY
B.Sc., Ph.D., F. Inst. P.

PROFESSOR OF PHYSICS, UNIVERSITY COLLEGE OF THE GOLD COAST

LONDON
MACMILLAN & CO LTD
NEW YORK · ST MARTIN'S PRESS
1954

MACMILLAN AND COMPANY LIMITED
London Bombay Calcutta Madras Melbourne

THE MACMILLAN COMPANY OF CANADA LIMITED
Toronto

ST MARTIN'S PRESS INC
New York

PRINTED IN GREAT BRITAIN

PREFACE

THE range of topics entitled to a place under the general head of Nuclear Physics is today so wide that, unless the discussion is superficial, it cannot be encompassed within the covers of a single book. It is therefore inevitable that certain natural divisions into which the subject falls should receive separate treatment. This entails some risk that the student, becoming interested in a limited region, will fail to see the wood for the trees ; and it happens that here the wood is worth seeing. He is therefore invited in these pages to take a more general view, to survey the family of nuclides as a whole, to attend not so much to individual nuclei as to the systematics of the nuclides and to general rules affecting the nuclear species as a group. As the chemist is trained to keep the Periodic Classification of the elements as a mental background of his work, so here the university student of nuclear physics is led to keep in mind a panoramic picture of the whole gamut of the nuclear species classified into ninety-six groups of isotopes. Such a broad view merits separate treatment not only as a necessary background of specialized studies but also for its intrinsic interest.

While the work is intended primarily for the aspirant to university honours in physics, it is hoped that the more advanced physicist will also find herein matter to interest him. To meet the needs of the student of chemistry who, while his work requires an acquaintance with nuclear physics, lacks the appropriate mathematical training, the approach to the subject has been as far as possible non-mathematical. An effort has been made to combine lucidity with brevity without sacrificing the precision of description and economy of nomenclature which is traditional in scientific writing. It is hoped, therefore, that these pages will provide a readable introduction to nuclear physics for students of both physics and chemistry. While the work cannot be classified as "popular science", it should be intelligible also to the layman with a scientific training. For those who wish to read further a list of references is provided.

It is a pleasure to record my gratitude to my colleague, Dr. A. H. Ward, for his valuable help in reading the proofs.

UNIVERSITY COLLEGE OF THE GOLD COAST   H. E. HUNTLEY
ACHIMOTA
GOLD COAST

CONTENTS

CONTENTS

INTRODUCTION

THE science of nuclear physics was born in 1896 when Henri
Becquerel discovered radioactivity. Since that year the rapidity
of its growth has been spectacular. This is true by whatever
yard-stick its rate of increase be measured. The volume of
original work in this branch of physics, as estimated by the
relative number of contributions to scientific journals, exceeds
that in any other branch of physics. The number of physicists
who are today occupied with nuclear physics studies are in a
large and increasing majority. In the first half of the twentieth
century more than half the Nobel prizes for physics were
awarded for discoveries in nuclear physics. The impact of the
new knowledge of the sub-atomic world upon industry, tech-
nology, medicine, methods of warfare and, indeed, upon physical
science itself is common knowledge. Pure mathematics provides an illustration. While no doubt it remains true that the
obligatory approximations of physics methods are anathema to
the pure mathematician, he would be the last to deny that the
history of mathematics has been significantly influenced by the
classical studies of the astronomer, the physicist and the astro-
physicist. That influence has been even more marked since the
study of the atom became the main preoccupation of physics.
To see the truth of this one has only to recall the impetus given
to the study of Riemann geometry by Einstein's relativity
theory, or of differential equations by the wave mechanics of
Schrödinger or of group theory by Heisenberg's quantum
mechanics. Theoretical chemistry provides another illustration
of the force of the impact of nuclear physics on other branches
of knowledge. For over half a century this subject has been the
growing point of physics until today its future course is a matter
of world-wide interest and, indeed, concern, for it is almost
universally realised that, from the secular standpoint, it can
make or mar the world. It may yet be within its power to raise

Western civilization to new high levels of health, prosperity and material welfare or to wipe it out and condemn mankind to a new experience of the Dark Ages.

It is well understood today that the application of some un-heralded scientific discovery in an obscure laboratory to the material environment of man may issue in a far-reaching amelioration of his resources and welfare. Faraday's discovery of the principle of the electric dynamo and Sir Alexander Fleming's discovery of penicillin are two examples among many. But it is not so widely realised that some scientific discoveries have a peculiar potency for transforming the human outlook—the *Weltanschauung* of mankind. A classical illustration of this is the revolutionary change in man's view of the universe which commenced with the birth of modern observational astronomy on 6th January, 1610 when Galileo Galilei first turned the newly invented telescope upon the night sky. Nuclear physics shows promise of effecting comparable changes in man's world-view. The Uncertainty Principle of Heisenberg is a very strange and novel notion which is having repercussions in the philosophy of science. Even more revolutionary is the doubt which certain experiments in nuclear physics have aroused concerning so sacrosanct a tenet as the Principle of Causality. The deter-minism of nineteenth-century physical science is not so secure as it seemed even three decades ago. This is not the place to embark upon a discussion of the philosophical implications of these fertile discoveries of nuclear physics. It is, however, worth while to remind the reader that this branch of science is destined not only to change the face of the world, for better or for worse, on the material plane : it will in all probability exert a decisive influence on scientific philosophy even to the point of transforming man's basic ideas of the universe in which he lives.

The full history of nuclear physics has yet to be written. It is to be found in the journals of the science. It is therefore useful at this point, in the interests of historical perspective and in the absence of a systematic account, to set down at least the important dates of major developments of the subject. This summary obviously cannot make any pretension to complete-ness. Selection is necessary in the interests of brevity.

Important Dates

Radioactivity

1896. H. Becquerel discovered radioactivity. Two years later Pierre and Marie Curie isolated radium.

1903. E. Rutherford and F. Soddy showed that radioactivity involved spontaneous transmutation of certain elements.

1934. F. and I. Curie-Joliot discovered artificial radioactivity by bombarding aluminium with α-particles. Since then over 700 nuclear species have been rendered artificially radioactive.

Particle Accelerators

1919. Rutherford produced the first nuclear reaction, the *first controlled transmutation*, by bombarding nitrogen with α-particles and transmuting it into oxygen. This pointed to the need for the artificial production of high energy particles.

1930. J. D. Cockcroft and E. T. S. Walton built the *first particle accelerator* and brought about the first artificial transmutation.

1931. R. J. Van de Graaff constructed a practical *electrostatic accelerator*.

1932. E. O. Lawrence built the *cyclotron*.

1945. E. M. McMillan (U.S.A.) and V. Veksler (U.S.S.R.) independently suggested the principle of the *synchroton*.

Detecting Instruments

1911. C. T. R. Wilson developed the *cloud chamber* for observing the tracks of ionizing particles.

1928. H. Geiger and W. Müller devised the *counter* now known by their name. This device in conjunction with a scaler is the most generally useful of the instruments used for nuclear physics measurements.

1939. C. F. Powell, in collaboration with Ilford, Ltd., developed the photographic emulsion into a means of estimating ionising particles. This " *nuclear emulsion* " has been invaluable in the study of cosmic radiation.

1947. H. Kallmann invented the *scintillation counter*. The combination of a zinc sulphide scintillation screen, as used 40 years earlier by Rutherford and co-workers, with an electron multiplier tube is the most efficient method of counting α-particles and γ-rays.

Nuclear Particles

1897. J. J. Thomson discovered the *electron*.

1899. E. Rutherford, simultaneously with others, found that two types of charged particles were emitted by uranium. He named them *alpha particles* and *beta particles*. The former were shown to be the nuclei of helium atoms, the latter electrons.

1900. P. Villard discovered *gamma rays*, electromagnetic radiation moving with the velocity of light.

1914. E. Rutherford discovered the *proton*.

1932. J. Chadwick discovered the *neutron* while repeating experiments of the Curie-Joliots.

1932. C. D. Anderson observed the *positron*, the existence of which had been postulated by P. A. M. Dirac for theoretical reasons.

1936. S. H. Neddermeyer and C. D. Anderson discovered the *meson*, a particle of mass $\sim 200\ m_e$ (m_e = mass of electron), as a component of cosmic rays.

1947. C. F. Powell and his colleagues discovered the *π-meson* in cosmic radiation. Its mass is about 300 m_e and it disintegrates spontaneously emitting a meson, now called a *μ-meson* of mass 200 m_e. Mesons of both types may have either positive or negative charges.

1948. E. Gardner and C. Lattes produced mesons by bombardment of carbon.

1950. P. M. S. Blackett announced the detection in cosmic radiation of particles of mass 1000 m_e approximately, one example of which C. F. Powell had found and named *τ-meson*.

Cosmic Rays

1911. V. G. Hess discovered cosmic rays. C. T. R. Wilson had shown that an unknown radiation discharged the most securely insulated electroscope and Hess proved that it originated from regions outside the earth.

1927. D. Skobelzyn employed a Wilson cloud chamber,

situated in a magnetic field, to study cosmic rays—a powerful combination.

1927. Clay discovered the *latitude effect*.

1929. W. Bothe and W. Kolhörster applied the Geiger-Müller tube to the study of cosmic rays.

1943. C. F. Powell commenced a fruitful research in this field by exposing nuclear emulsions to cosmic rays on high mountain peaks and, later, in balloons retained at pre-arranged heights.

1936. Discovery of the *mesons* by Neddermeyer and Anderson

1947. and by Powell (see above).

1948. United States investigators found that heavy particles are constituents of the primary cosmic rays.

Theory

1905. A. Einstein published his restricted theory of relativity, the *mass-energy equivalence* being a corollary.

1911/3. E. Rutherford and N. Bohr published the hypothesis of the *nuclear atom*.

1926. E. Schrödinger introduced *wave mechanics* based on the wave-particle duality of matter.

1927. W. Heisenberg proposed the *Uncertainty Principle*, a generalization of great significance.

1932. W. Heisenberg proposed the hypothesis that *atomic nuclei are built of protons and neutrons*, mutually attracted by exchange forces.

Nuclear Power

1939. O. Hahn and F. Strassmann discovered *nuclear fission*.

1942. E. Fermi, at the head of a team of scientific workers in unprecedented numbers, inaugurated *the first pile* for the production of nuclear power, etc.

1945. *The atomic bomb*.

1951. First production of electric current by nuclear energy.

Unclassified Dates

1913. J. J. Thomson discovered stable isotopes.

1919. F. W. Aston built the first accurate mass spectrograph.

1932. H. C. Urey and his collaborators discovered deuterium and heavy water.

1937. I. I. Rabi studied nuclear moments by means of micro-waves.

In the foregoing lists of dates it may be noticed that the war years 1939 to 1945 appear to have been unfruitful. The fact is, of course, precisely the opposite. Never before in the history of science have so many physicists been organized for discovery and invention as in the years of the second world war. Their activities, in the United States, the United Kingdom, Canada and Australia, ranged over the whole field of nuclear physics, but they had a single aim, the control of nuclear power, and the production of a bomb of unprecedented efficacy. The remark-able story has been well told by H. D. Smyth (1945). But the military value of discoveries in the realm of nuclear physics were so obvious that Security Regulations of the strictest order were imposed on their nationals by all the warring nations. The spate of published research was reduced to a trickle.

Political Effects

The secrecy imposed in time of war is still enforced in days of peace. The continuance of the application of Security Regula-tions in all countries engaged in nuclear research is not the least important of the changes brought about by the new science. From the point of view of the progress of physical science the veto on publication of new knowledge is an unmitigated evil. In the nineteenth century there was a pleasant international rivalry among scientists. The pooling of knowledge was tradi-tional. Discovery and invention, hypothesis and theory were published widely and freely. This international fraternity and co-operation in the great cause of wresting her secrets from Nature was a source of gratification and pride among scientific workers of all nations. The situation today is very different. Today, a man who ventured to publish to the world some new discovery of real value in nuclear physics would be regarded as unpatriotic. Civil servants engaged in such studies are under the strictest pledge of secrecy. It is easy to see how this change in the international character of physical science puts a brake on progress. Apart from the sad truth that the happy spirit of international co-operation between physical scientists has been replaced by something like a " cold war ", there is the deplorable

waste of effort resulting from the duplication of experiments
even in countries that are on terms of friendship, the refusal to
share " key " materials and the suppression by statute of the
publication of important results of research. This is not a political pamphlet and it would be inappropriate to " point the
moral " ; it is sufficient to emphasise that, apart from its social
effects, the development of nuclear science has instigated
political supervision and this has had a deplorable influence
upon international co-operation and upon the *tempo* of scientific
progress.

Natural Divisions of Nuclear Physics

The scope of this subject is now so wide that it is no longer
possible to provide within the limits of one volume anything
more than an emaciated version of all the topics that are rightly
included under this heading. Whatever may have been the case
in the past, it is certain that in the future the vast area of nuclear
physics for didactic purposes must be subdivided, each subdivision receiving treatment in a separate treatise. The tendency is becoming more obvious today. This book is evidence
of this growing necessity. The reader will find that, while no
sub-topic in these pages is exhaustively dealt with, the area of
nuclear physics covered in these pages is nevertheless severely
restricted. Although the aim is a general view of the whole
family of nuclides, those aspects of the nuclear species which are
related to *mass* and *binding energy* are the only major topics
discussed ; but it will become clear as we proceed that this does
in fact form a natural and inevitable division of the subject,
susceptible of integrated study without much reference to other
natural divisions. A clear sign of this circumscription is the fact
that the subject matter is centred on the experimental results
from *one* instrument—the mass spectrograph, and the theoretical consequences of *one* basic hypothesis—the mass-energy
equivalence of Einstein. These experimental results and this
hypothesis are fundamental to the natural division of the subject
which is set out in the following pages. For those readers who
are interested in the early origins of scientific knowledge it may
be remarked that practically the whole subject matter of this
book can be traced back to two items of new knowledge, viz.,

the discovery of *kanalstrahlen* and the formulation of the theory of relativity.

In 1886 Goldstein observed that when the cathode of a discharge tube was pierced by a small hole, a glowing streamer was to be seen on the side of the cathode opposed to the anode. The canalised rays were at first called kanalstrahlen. When, however, it was shown that they consisted of positively charged particles they were given the name of *positive rays*. It was soon understood that the positive rays were positive ions which were attracted to the cathode. Those that passed through the perforation ionised the residual rarefied gas and produced a glow of light. In 1911 Sir J. J. Thomson undertook a quantitative examination of the phenomenon. One of the consequences of his work was the mass spectrograph (Chap. III).

In 1905 A. Einstein published his Restricted Theory of Relativity. It was the outcome of an attempt to find an explanation of the negative result of Michelson and Morley's experiment to determine a change in the velocity of light due to the changing relative motion of the earth and the ether. Einstein abandoned the ether hypothesis and made two postulates : first, that the velocity of light is a constant which is independent of the motion of either the observer or the source, and second, that it is impossible to measure " absolute velocity ". Einstein's theory has had a profound influence upon all branches of physical science. In relation to the topic of nuclear mass and energy, one revolutionary result of Einstein's work should be noted here. The nineteenth-century belief in the conservation of mass has had to be abandoned. The observed mass of a body was shown to be a function of its velocity relative to the observer. Moreover, there is an equivalence of mass and energy which is capable of simple quantitative expression. This is discussed in Chap. VII. The increase of mass with velocity is shown graphically in Fig. 0.1. If m_0 is the mass of a particle at rest and m is its mass when moving relative to the observer with a velocity v, the graph shows the increase of the ratio m/m_0 as the ratio v/c increases, c being the velocity of light. It will be observed that the increase of mass is very rapid when v exceeds $0.9\ c$.

On these two scientific discoveries, then—one experimental,

re, has not been set out in ordered array before. Mass
ects and binding energies (Chaps. VI and VII) should also be
ken together as forming a single, indivisible topic ; one,
oreover, of fundamental importance. Chap. VIII on isobars
s of interest partly on account of the light it sheds on the subject of decay by β-emission and K-capture. An account of a
remarkable equation, usually known as the *Mass Equation*,
which has a semi-empirical origin, and the relative contributions of experiment and theory to its formulation are set out in
Chap. IX. The subject of the " Magic Numbers ", discussed in
Chap. X, is in a stage of immaturity. The interested reader is
referred to current physics journals for further information.
The age of the elements (Chap. XII) is a matter of great interest.
It was shown by Goldschmidt (1938) that the relative natural
abundance of the elements was related to nuclear mass (*v.* Fig.
12.1) and hence to the stability line of the isotopic chart. A
short account of the age and possible origin of the elements
provides therefore an appropriate conclusion to a review of the
mass and stability of nuclear species.

To conclude this Introduction a cautionary word to the
junior student who is reading nuclear physics for the first time
may perhaps be permitted. It concerns what, in the author's
view, is the proper mental attitude towards the subject. While
this book has been written primarily for Sixth Form pupils and
University undergraduates who expect to read for an Honours
degree in physics, a larger class of readers—as was mentioned
in the Preface—has been kept in mind and an effort has been
made to provide an account of nuclear mass and energy which
would be intelligible to graduates in sciences other than physics.
But this must not be understood to imply that this is a work of
" popular science ". The reader who hopes to find an account
of the exciting practical applications of nuclear physics—
" tagged atoms ", nuclear power, the atom bomb, etc.—will be
disappointed. Not that such applications are irrelevant. But
these are the fruits, and our business here is with the roots of the
subject. The subject matter of the following pages is basic, not
applied, nuclear physics. That being so, the reader who is
disciplined to appreciate the austere attitude of the physicist to
his subject should experience *aesthetic pleasure* as he reads.

the other theoretical—is based that b...
which forms the subject matter of the...

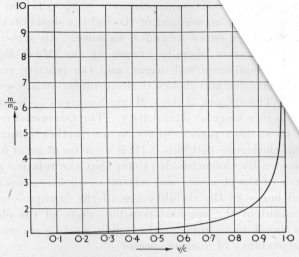

FIG. 0.1. Increase of mass with velocity.

other experiment and no other theory of comparable importance is invoked.

A final theory of nuclear constitution has not yet been formulated. Some information concerning the size and possible structure of the nucleus is, however, set out in Chaps. II and X. Is the structure simple? Gamow quotes Lord Rutherford (1931) as saying, " It is my personal conviction that if we knew more about the nucleus, we should find it much simpler than we suppose ". The only appropriate comment, twenty years later, is that, apparently, we have not yet garnered sufficient knowledge to reveal the simplicity, although the understanding of nuclear structure and inter-nucleonic forces is a major aim of present-day physics. The discovery, the nature, and the artificial separation of stable isotopes is the topic of Chap. III. In Chapter IV is found the *ZN* diagram which is of basic importance. Chapters IV and V should be regarded as one whole, divided for convenience into two sections. They deal with the *Systematics of the Nuclides*, a topic that, as far as the author is

B   H.N.S.

Whether he does or does not, it remains true that the author, in writing this introduction to one branch of nuclear science, has been animated by a single desire to behold beauty and to set it out in order for the enjoyment of physics students and others. It is hoped that readers in both classes may derive from reading these pages not merely factual knowledge but also the pure pleasures of aesthetic appreciation.

REFERENCES

V. M. Goldschmidt, 1938, *Verteilungsgesetze der Elemente.*

E. Rutherford, 1931, *Göttingen Lecture.*

H. D. Smyth, 1945, *Atomic Energy for Military Purposes,* Princetown University Press.

CHAPTER I

THE ATOMIC NUCLEUS

In 1896 Becquerel found that radiation from uranium was capable of fogging a photographic plate. During the half century that has elapsed since that momentous observation not a year has passed which has failed to add new knowledge to the garnered store of information relating to the nucleus of the atom. Today the spate of papers is so great that editors of scientific journals can print only the most important contributions and publication of many of these usually suffers considerable delay. Nuclear physics is one of the chief growing points of Science and the rate of growth is increasing annually. This acceleration is itself a major phenomenon ; nothing to compare with it has been seen in the history of Science. It will accordingly be obvious that it would be absurd to endeavour to give an account of the atomic nucleus within the bounds of a single chapter without assuming that a large background of knowledge was already in the possession of the reader. Even so, the most that can be attempted is to provide an outline of a few of the main facts which find general acceptance today among physicists and this for the most part without attempting a chronological sequence of discovery or a justification of accepted views. The reader should also remember that in studying the nucleus he is on the shadowy verge which separates knowledge and ignorance. After half a century of research into its nature, the nucleus still holds most of its secrets. Little is understood of its constitution and less of the forces that control it. There is, however, one advance in understanding accruing from the study of the atom and its nucleus which is of great interest and importance to the natural philosopher. It is that in the subatomic world we are out of our mental depth in the sense that the human mind, accustomed as it is only to macroscopic scenes and images, cannot function by the use of its imaginative faculty in the microscopic world where pictures and models as analogues are, in general, as inappropriate as they are misleading. This mental limitation is becoming clearer with every passing year ; it leads to the expectation that the future faithful representation of the nucleus will consist of nothing more illuminating than a series of mathematical equations.

Becquerel's discovery aroused the interest of a Polish lady, Marie Curie, and later of a New Zealander, Ernest Rutherford— two of the greatest names in nuclear physics. Madame Curie isolated polonium and radium from tons of ore and thus provided Rutherford indirectly with the ammunition, the α-particles, with which he bombarded metal foils, experiments which led him to the theory of the nuclear atom which is now universally accepted. Incidentally, it was the α-particle, also, which played a major rôle in the discovery of the neutron and of induced radioactivity.

Rutherford's model of the atom superseded the tentative hypothesis of Sir J. J. Thomson who conceived the atom to consist of " a number of corpuscles [electrons] moving about in a sphere of uniform positive electrification ". He added : " the corpuscles will arrange themselves in a series of concentric shells ", thus anticipating Bohr's model. This atom was of course electrically neutral, but the concept of a sphere of positive electrification was vague. A Hungarian, Lenard, in 1903 proposed a model in which the positive sphere in which electrons were embedded was replaced by a small massive nucleus at the centre of an electric field of force. A Japanese, Nagaoka, in 1904 compared an atom with Saturn and his rings. But it was left to Rutherford and his colleagues to establish the nuclear theory of the atom on a sound experimental basis.

As early as 1906 Rutherford, then at McGill University, Canada, observed that α-particles passing through metal foil before falling on a photographic plate gave rise to an image which was diffuse at the edges. This was attributed to the deflection of the particles by the atoms of the foil. Three years later Rutherford, now in Manchester University, with Geiger and Marsden, undertook a series of classic experiments which laid the foundation of the theory of the nuclear atom. It was observed first that α-particles could pass through a metal foil

thousands of atoms thick without being deflected. Large
deviations from the original path of the bombarding particle
occurred so rarely that the conclusion was reasonable that the
field of force producing the deflections was of very small
dimensions. Very rarely an incident α-particle was deflected
through more than 90°. This happened to about one particle
in ten thousand. The event astonished Rutherford, who remarked that it was " as credible as if you had fired a 15-inch
shell at a piece of tissue paper and it came back and hit you ".
Using these observations Rutherford verified his scattering
formula which is referred to in Chap. II (p. 21). This formula
led to the surprising conclusion, fundamental in nuclear physics,
that practically the whole mass of the atom is concentrated
within a volume a million million times smaller than that of the
atom. As we shall see in the next chapter, the radius of the
nucleus is between 10^{-12} and 10^{-13} cm. The foregoing considerations point to the " emptiness " of the atom and account
for the observation that an α-particle, which is electrically
charged, can pass through many thousands of atoms without
being deflected. Rutherford later showed that the α-particle
was the nucleus of the helium atom, that is, the helium atom
minus its two orbital electrons. Its mass is 6.65×10^{-24} gm.
This leads to the conclusion that the density of nuclear matter is
about 100,000 tons per cubic millimetre ! It will be noticed that
even in its earliest beginnings the advance of nuclear physics
waited upon the development of experimental resources, the
bombarding particles and the means of detecting nuclear
radiations. That has remained true. For the first three decades, the only ammunition of the nuclear physicist was that
derived from natural sources, the α-particles, β-particles and
γ-rays of naturally radioactive elements. Since 1930 when
Cockcroft and Walton produced the first artificially accelerated
particles there has been a vast development of particle accelerators of different types, including the Van de Graaff electrostatic
generator, the cyclotron, the betatron, the linear accelerator
and the synchrotron. The particle energies thus artificially
produced, while greatly exceeding those from radioactive
sources, are still short of those found in the cosmic radiation.
Although the enormous field of artificial radioactivity was

opened up by means of naturally produced α-particles—in 1934, when Irene Curie and her husband, F. Joliot were studying the effects of bombarding aluminium with α-particles—its extension to what promises to become a major branch of physics has been principally due to the development of ever more powerful particle accelerators.

On the other hand the principal instruments for detecting nuclear particles were in use in the early days. By 1913 four different instruments were employed, all of which depended for their functioning on the fact that a nuclear particle in its swift passage through matter produced *ionisation*. By stripping the atoms which lay in its path of one or more of its orbital electrons the swiftly moving particle produced large numbers of positively charged ions and free electrons, the presence of which could be revealed in different ways. The four instruments of detection in historical order of application are the photographic plate, the scintillation screen, the Geiger counter and the Wilson cloud chamber. This is not the place to give an account of these instruments, but it is worth noting how great has been the improvement in the sensitivity as well as in the reliability and convenience in use of each of them. The " nuclear emulsion " photographic plate of today, invented by C. F. Powell (1946) and perfected by Ilford, Ltd. and later by Kodak, Ltd. will detect any particle producing a minimum ionisation. The scintillation screen has grown into the scintillation counter, suitable luminescent crystals in conjunction with electron multipliers being employed to operate " scalers " counting hundreds of thousands of particles per minute. This is probably the best method of counting α-particles. The combination of Geiger counters and Wilson cloud chambers by Blackett and others has proved to be one of the most powerful means of studying nuclear reactions and cosmic radiation.

The Nuclear Charge

In 1913, Moseley, working in Rutherford's laboratory, using a crystal as a diffraction grating, investigated the X-ray spectra of a large number of elements and found that the wavelength of the principal line of X-ray spectra, K_α, became successively shorter in a regular manner in passing from elements of low to elements of higher atomic number, in the order of the chemical classification. This regularity could be expressed by the relation

$$\nu = c/\lambda = \text{const. } (Z-1)^2 \qquad (1.1)$$

where Z is the atomic number of the element. Moseley's conclusion was of great importance. He wrote : " . . . we have here a proof that there is in the atom a fundamental quantity, which increases by regular steps as we pass from one element to the next. This quantity can only be the charge on the atomic nucleus . . . We are therefore led to the view that [the charge on the nucleus] is the same as the number of the place occupied by the element in the periodic system. This atomic number is then for hydrogen 1 ; for helium 2, for lithium 3 . . . " Some time later Van den Broek confirmed that Moseley's " atomic number " was identical with the charge Z on the nucleus and further confirmation came from accurate experiments on the scattering of α-particles made in 1920 in Rutherford's laboratory in Cambridge.

This result today is one of the basic assumptions of nuclear physics : the positive charge carried by the nucleus of an element is numerically equal to the atomic number of that element. Consequently, since the atom is electrically neutral, the atomic number is equal to the number of orbital electrons. Thus, the symbol Z stands for the value of the positive charge on the nucleus, the atomic number and the number of orbital electrons. Hydrogen, has for example atomic number 1, unit charge on the nucleus and one orbital electron : uranium has atomic number 92, its nucleus has 92 positive charges and 92 orbital electrons.

The Neutron

From the early days the possibility of a nuclear particle of zero charge $(Z=0)$ was discussed. In 1920 Rutherford said " . . . it may be possible for an electron to combine much more closely with the hydrogen nucleus forming a kind of neutral doublet. . . . Its external field would be practically zero . . . Its presence would probably be difficult to detect ". This particle was first observed but not recognised in 1930. Bothe and Becker found that when certain elements of low atomic number, notably beryllium, were bombarded with α-particles, radiation of high penetrating power, thought to be γ-radiation, was produced. In 1932, Joliot and Joliot-Curie found that when the radiation fell on paraffin wax, protons of high energy were ejected. Chadwick, in the same year, identified this radiation, showing that it consisted of particles of mass nearly equal to that of the proton and with no net charge. The particle was called the *neutron*. Since its charge is zero it is not an ionising particle and therefore its presence cannot be revealed by the four methods of detection described above. It may be detected by its power to expel protons from hydrogenous material and also by its interaction with atomic nuclei of which that of boron is an example. The irradiation of boron with neutrons produces α-particles in accordance with the nuclear reaction (Chap. III, p. 53) :

$$^{10}_{5}B + n \rightarrow {}^{7}_{3}Li + {}^{4}_{2}He$$

The lithium and helium nuclei share an energy of $2\frac{1}{2}$ million electron volts. Thus a Geiger counter which contains boron will detect neutrons by means of the ionisation produced by the α-particles.

The discovery of the neutron has proved to be a major event in the history of nuclear physics. The neutron is regarded as a fundamental unit of nuclear structure ; it reacts with every species of nucleus and is accordingly an indispensable tool of nuclear chemistry ; and it unlocked the door to the production of atomic energy. In these pages we are concerned with the neutron primarily as one of the building bricks of the nucleus.

Nuclear Structure

For many years before the discovery of the neutron in 1932 the nucleus was assumed to contain closely packed protons each having unit mass on the atomic scale and carrying unit positive charge. The stability of this system of mutually repelling electrostatic charges remained unexplained. Since the atomic number Z is the same as the nuclear charge and this is about half the atomic mass A, it was necessary to assume that $A - Z$ of the proton charges were neutralised by the presence in the nucleus of $A - Z$ electrons. Although the presence of these nuclear electrons might account for the emission of β-particles by unstable nuclei, certain difficulties presented themselves which became increasingly intractable. The discovery of the neutron led Heisenberg to suggest a resolution of the difficulties by assuming that the two principal constituents of the nucleus were the proton and the neutron. The term *nucleon* is used today as a generic title for both particles. Heisenberg, using the new wave mechanics, also showed that the stability of nuclei might be accounted for by " exchange forces ", a type of wave mechanical attractive force which had been used to account for the stability of molecules containing two or more atoms. β-particles emitted by a radioactive nucleus are assumed to be manufactured during the decay process, possibly by the conversion of a neutron into a proton :

$$n \rightarrow p + \beta^- \tag{1.3}$$

On this basis the nuclei of the first six elements might be schematically represented by the configuration of Fig. 1.1.

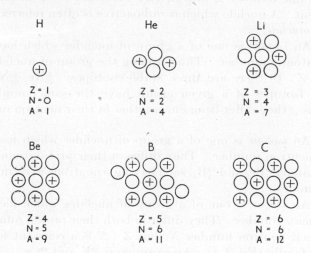

FIG. 1.1. Nucleons in simple nuclides

In 1816 an English scientist, William Prout, had suggested that all atomic masses might be integral multiples of the masses of the hydrogen atom. It is known today that the masses of most atoms do approximate to whole numbers on a scale in which the mass of the proton is unity. If A, called the *mass number*, is the nearest integer to the mass of a nucleus containing Z protons and N neutrons,

$$Z + N = A \tag{1.4}$$

It is appropriate at this point to refer to some other terms and symbols which are in current use in nuclear physics.

(1) The term *nuclide* is coming into use to designate a nuclear species, that is, an atomic species characterized by its nuclear constitution. It is represented by the chemical symbol (X) of the element with superscript (A) denoting the mass number and a subscript (Z) denoting the atomic number : $_Z^A X$. Thus, $_9^{19}F$ is the nuclide fluorine, of which the atomic number is 9 and the mass number is 19. From Eq. (1.4) it is evident that the nucleus of this nuclide contains 10 neutrons. If it is desired to state explicitly the number of neutrons in a nucleus, a second subscript is used: $_9^{19}F_{10}$. Since the letter designates the nuclide, the atomic number is not strictly necessary ; ^{19}F is formally sufficient. A nuclide which is radioactive is often referred to as a *radionuclide*.

(2) An *isotope* is one of a group of nuclides which have the same atomic number. Thus, among the group of nuclides for which $Z = 10$ there are three stable isotopes : $_{10}^{20}Ne$, $_{10}^{21}Ne$ and $_{10}^{22}Ne$. Isotopes of a given group have the same number of protons ; they differ from one another in their neutron number N.

(3) An *isotone* is one of a group of nuclides which have the same neutron number. They differ in their proton number Z. For example $_4^9Be_5$ and $_5^{10}B_5$, each having 5 neutrons in its nucleus, are isotones.

(4) An *isobar* is one of a group of nuclides which have the same mass number. They differ in both their proton number Z and their neutron number N, but $Z + N$ is a constant for any isobar family (Eq. 1.4). An example is $_{19}^{40}K$ and $_{20}^{40}Ca$.

(5) An *isomer* is one of two nuclides which have the same atomic number, the same neutron number and therefore the same mass number. They can be distinguished only by the fact that they exist in different energy levels (*v.* Chap. XI). $_{35}^{80}Br$ and $_{35}^{80}Br^*$ are isomers, the asterisk indicating that the

nuclide exists in an excited state which is metastable. The excited state can continue for periods which vary with different isomers from seconds to years.

The significance of these terms is illuminated by a method of representing the nuclides, which (including the radionuclides) number over one thousand, by means of a chart. In this the atomic numbers Z are set out as abscissae and the neutron numbers N as ordinates. In this book such a chart is of basic importance. It will often be referred to as the ZN *diagram*. One ZN diagram, which charts the stable nuclides only, is found in Chap. IV (Fig. 4.1). Another, which includes all the known nuclides, is in Chap. V (Fig. 5.1). The reader to whom this method of representation is new should examine these diagrams with care and should then consider the foregoing definitions in relation to them.

Stability of the Nucleus

The accurate measurement of the masses of the nuclei leads to a knowledge of their relative stability. The mass measurements are made by means of the mass spectrograph, an instrument originated by Sir J. J. Thomson and developed by F. W. Aston (Chap. III). This instrument is of fundamental importance in relation to the subject matter of these pages. Its data are interpreted by means of a theoretical result of similar basic importance in the same reference, viz. the mass-energy equivalence. In 1905 Einstein, as one of the results of his special relativity theory, derived the equation

$$E = mc^2 \tag{1.5}$$

where E is the energy equivalent of a mass m and c is the velocity of light. One gram of matter is thus equivalent to $(3 \times 10^{10})^2$ ergs of energy. The relevance of this to nuclear stability may be seen by considering the helium nucleus or α-particle. This contains two protons of mass 2·01516 and two neutrons of mass 2·01794, total 4·03310 mass units. The unit of mass (amu or mu) is 1/16th of the mass of the neutral oxygen atom $^{16}_{8}O$, one of the isotopes of oxygen, which is fixed at 16·000000. But the mass of the α-particle is only 4·0028 mu. Thus the combination of the four nuclei to form an α-particle involves a loss of mass of 0·0303 mu called the *mass defect*, which by Eq. (1.5) is equivalent to a loss of energy of $4·5 \times 10^{-5}$ ergs or 28·2 MeV. Conversely, to break up an α-particle into its constituent nucleons would necessitate the supply of this relatively large amount of energy, which is called the *binding energy* of the nucleus. It is clear that binding energy, being the amount of energy required completely to dissociate the nucleus into its constituent nucleons, is a measure of the stability of the nucleus relative to this particular mode of dissociation. It should not be forgotten, however, that there are other modes of division of a nucleus and these may require a smaller contribution of energy. It is found that the binding energy of nuclei increases with atomic number to a maximum in the neighbourhood of $Z = 56$, and then slowly diminishes (Chap. VII, Fig. 7.3, p. 117).

Exchange Forces

The nature of the forces which bind the nucleons together to form a stable nucleus is still an unsolved problem. The positively charged nuclear protons, instead of sticking together, might be expected to repel one another with violence. A somewhat similar problem had faced the chemist who had to explain the mutual attraction of two hydrogen atoms to form a stable molecule. This attractive force was brilliantly accounted for on the basis of quantum mechanical considerations. That memorable success is properly regarded as one of the greatest achievements of quantum mechanics. Unfortunately an understanding of the nature of the attractive force requires a greater knowledge of quantum mechanics than is expected from most readers of these pages. It may, however, be briefly referred to. It is assumed that a proton and neutron which are adjacent to one another in a nucleus exchange their roles many times per second by the transfer of a particle carrying the electric charge, the proton becoming a neutron and the neutron becoming a proton. The energy of the system after the exchange is the same as before. The system can thus exist in two states having the same energy. In such a case the actual state of the system is a combination of the two states and has a greater stability ; that is, energy has been added. It is called an *exchange force.* This force is operative only over very short distances. Its effective range is less than the diameter of a nucleus of medium size. This accounts for the fact that, whereas the radius of an atom is a somewhat indefinite quantity, that of a nucleus is sharply defined. The coulomb repulsive force between two protons increases much less rapidly with decreasing separation, so that the net force between protons— the p-p force—is attractive at short distances.

What is the nature of the particle assumed in this theory to be exchanged between two nucleons? Like the positive electron, it was postulated by the theorist before its existence was revealed by experiment. For various reasons it was clear that the exchange particle could not be an electron and in 1934 a Japanese physicist, Yukawa, showed that a particle having about 140 times the mass of an electron would meet the requirements of theory. To account for β-decay he also stated that the particle would be an electron emitter with a half-life of 10^{-6} seconds. Yukawa's theory attracted little attention until two years later when physicists studying cosmic radiation discovered particles having a mass of about 200 times that of the electron. This " heavy electron ", being intermediate in mass between the electron and the proton, is called the *meson*. It was found to be unstable, an electron emitter of short half-life—about $2 \cdot 15 \mu$ sec.

The approximate equality in the magnitude of the p-p, n-n and p-n nuclear forces suggests that mesons may be positively or negatively charged or neutral. The existence of particles of all three varieties is today well established. Mesons of natural origin are not only encountered in routine cosmic ray studies but they are artificially produced by the more powerful of the particle accelerators. Nevertheless, a satisfactory theory of nuclear forces is still wanting. A number of different particles called *mesons*—π-meson, μ-meson, τ-meson, etc.—have been discovered in cosmic radiation, but the state of knowledge of these particles of intermediate mass and of the relations between them is still somewhat confused. It seems probable that the resolution of the current difficulties of the theoretical nuclear physicist must wait for the garnering of new and accurate information from the laboratories.

Nuclear Energy Levels

The notion of energy levels has become familiar through the study of the orbital electrons which can exist in different " states ". There is also evidence of the existence of energy levels within the nucleus, but these are not so well understood. The subject is discussed in Chap. X. We shall find that nuclei can exist in a quantum state above the ground state and that the transition from the higher to the lower energy state is accompanied by the radiation of a quantum of energy ; usually a γ-ray is emitted, the wave-length indicating the difference in the nuclear energy levels. The mean lifetime of an excited nucleus is between 10^{-17} and 10^{-13} sec., compared with 10^{-8} sec. for an excited atom. But, as we have seen, some nuclei can exist in a state of higher energy for a time varying from seconds to years. These are the *isomers*, of which over seventy examples have been found in recent years (Chap. XI).

It is believed that the nucleons of a nucleus in the ground state exist in *groups* in different energy levels and that the Pauli Exclusion Principle may determine the grouping. It is well known that a special degree of stability belongs to nuclides which contain 2, 8, 20, 50, 82 and 126 nucleons. Some progress has been made with a *nuclear shell* theory which accounts for these so-called " magic numbers " on the basis of the Exclusion Principle.

This topic is developed in Chap. X, where the representation of energy levels of the nuclide ^{8}Li (Fig. 10.3) gives an idea of the great complexity of nuclear energy levels. Since the experimental information is still far from complete it is clear that, unless some great generalization is discovered, the work of measuring and cataloguing energy levels of all nuclides will not be finished for many years to come. In the same chapter is found also an empirical explanation of the magic numbers and a tentative outline of a model of the nucleus which supposes that the nucleus contains a succession of " shells " analogous to those associated with the orbital electron structure.

Nuclear Spin

Like an atom, a nucleus has an angular momentum. This is made up of the vector sum of the angular momenta of the orbital motion of its nucleons compounded with the angular momenta resulting from their spinning on their own axes. The vector sum has been given the unsatisfactory name of *nuclear spin*. The spin of a nucleus in an excited state may differ from its spin in the ground state. Experimental methods of high sensitivity have been developed for measuring the spins of nuclei. The evidence shows that a nucleus has an angular momentum given by

$$s = \sqrt{I\,(I+1)} \cdot \frac{h}{2\pi} \qquad (1.6)$$

where I is called the *spin quantum number* or, more briefly, the *spin*. It is found that the spin quantum number of the proton and of the neutron is $\frac{1}{2}$. All the results to date show a remarkable correlation between the mass number A and the spin which may be stated thus :

(*a*) Nuclides with A even have integral spins.
(*b*) Nuclides with A odd have half-integral spins.

The rule constitutes part of the evidence that the early proton-electron theory of nuclear structure is untenable. This may be seen from an example. On this theory $^{14}_{7}N$ should contain 21 particles—14 protons and 7 electrons—and should therefore, since protons and electrons have half-integral spins, have a half-integral spin due to the odd electron. The spin of $^{14}_{7}N$, however, is integral in accordance with the rule.

Another rule, to which no exception has so far been found, is that nuclei containing even numbers of protons and neutrons have zero spin. It thus seems reasonable to suppose that in other nuclei the spin may be due to the odd particle. In these the spin quantum numbers are $\frac{1}{2}, \frac{3}{2}, \frac{5}{2}, \frac{7}{2}$ and $\frac{9}{2}$. No higher spin has been found.

It may be supposed that there is a pairing of spins of opposite signs for protons and for neutrons so that a nucleus containing an even number of nucleons will have zero spins. It is to be expected for the same reason that odd-odd nuclei would have integral spins and this is found to be so. Moreover, the odd-even and even-odd nuclei have half integral spins. It may be noted that, as a general rule, the members of a family of stable

C

isotopes have the same spin. This is a consequence of the foregoing rule together with rule 4 of Chap. IV (p. 70).

Theory shows that the probability of transition of a nucleus from one energy state to another depends on the change of spin. If the spin change is zero or unity the transition probability is high : the transition is " permitted ". If, however, a larger change of spin is involved the transition probability diminishes ; it is " forbidden " in a greater or less degree. These considerations have application to the phenomena of nuclear isomerism and metastable states (Chap. XI).

Nuclear Magnetism

Although the topic is not strictly relevant to the main subject matter of this book some account of nuclear magnetism is given here for the sake of completeness.

A particle carrying an electric charge which is revolving round a fixed point constitutes a circular electric current and possesses in consequence a magnetic moment. It may also have a magnetic moment as a result of rotation on its own axis. The amount of this magnetic moment may be crudely calculated from a classical physics argument as follows.

A charge e moving in a circular orbit of radius r with frequency $\omega/2\pi$ will have a magnetic moment

$$\mu = \text{current in e m u} \times \text{area enclosed}$$

$$= \frac{\omega}{2\pi} \cdot \frac{e}{c} \times \pi r^2 = \frac{e}{c} \cdot \frac{\omega r^2}{2}.$$

Since the angular momentum is quantized, $m\omega r^2 = \frac{nh}{2\pi}$. Hence

$$\mu = n \frac{eh}{4\pi mc}. \tag{1.7}$$

For an electron (mass m_e) the quantum

$$\mu_B = \frac{eh}{4\pi m_e c}$$

is called a Bohr magneton. But for a proton the corresponding unit is the nuclear magneton and is 1847 times smaller in value since the mass of the proton is 1847 m_e.

From wave mechanical arguments, the angular momentum

of a single particle is $2\sqrt{I(I+1)}$, where I is the spin quantum number. Hence, from Eq. (1.7) its magnetic moment is

$$= 2\sqrt{I(I+1)} \cdot \frac{e\hbar}{2mc} \cdot \quad \left(\hbar \equiv \frac{h}{2\pi} \right). \tag{1.8}$$

For an electron $I = \frac{1}{2}$ and the magnetic moment is therefore 1·732 Bohr magnetons. This is found to accord with experiment. On the other hand, the magnetic moment of a proton turns out to be not 1·732 but 2·79 nuclear magnetons. The neutron has a net charge equal to zero, but it must be presumed to contain separate charges of opposite sign because its magnetic moment, as found by experiment, is − 1·91 nuclear magnetons. The value is negative because its direction is opposite to that of the spin.

Since 1935 the experimental methods for measuring magnetic moments of nuclei have been developed along three independent lines associated with names of Bloch, Purcell and Rabi. They will not be described here. It must suffice to say that they have been brought to a high pitch of precision, the proton magnetic moment, for example, being known to an accuracy of one part in a hundred thousand. This compares favourably with the accuracy of mass spectrographic measurements. It is to be expected that the accumulation of measurements of such precision will lead to a better understanding of the nuclear fields of force.

Nuclear Transmutation

To transform a base metal into gold was a dream of the alchemists. It was not until 1919, however, that the first news was published of the transmutation of one element into another. Rutherford then showed that the bombardment of nitrogen with α-particles resulted in the production of protons of high energy. His results were confirmed and extended during the next five years by Chadwick. This historic nuclear reaction can be written after the fashion of a chemical equation :

$$^{14}_{7}\text{N} + ^{4}_{2}\text{He} \rightarrow ^{1}_{1}\text{H} + ^{17}_{8}\text{O} \tag{1.9}$$

It may be more succinctly expressed in a conventional manner thus :

$$^{14}\text{N} \; (\alpha, \, p) \; ^{17}\text{O}$$

An even briefer notation is in use : $^{14}\text{N} \cdot \alpha p$.

This contains all the necessary information since the total number of protons and the number of neutrons is unchanged. Mass, however, is not conserved. If the total initial and final masses of the nuclei involved in Eq. (1.9) are Σm_i and Σm_f then

$$Q = \Sigma m_i - \Sigma m_f$$

where Q is the net quantity of energy which has been created or destroyed according to whether m_i is greater or less than m_f. In the former case the reaction is said to be *exoergic*, in the latter *endoergic*.

In 1932 the first nuclear transmutation by artificially accelerated particles was achieved by Cockcroft and Walton in the Cavendish laboratory. They disintegrated lithium by irradiating it with protons of high energy. The products were two α-particles :

$$^7\text{Li}(p, \alpha)^4\text{He}$$

Since then particle accelerators of great power and of several types have brought about a very large number of nuclear transmutations, using a variety of bombarding particles. The most energetic of disintegrating particles are found in the cosmic radiation and these are now used in the study of nuclear reactions. Hundreds of nuclides produced by these processes are radioactive ; the study of their induced radioactivity has become a very wide subject of research.

It will be evident from the foregoing that the topic of nuclear transmutations constitutes in itself a very large branch of nuclear physics which might be appropriately discussed in a separate volume in three parts : (i) The reactions themselves are the basis of a new science, *nuclear chemistry* ; (ii) the products of disintegration, an extremely wide topic, are studied under the heading of *radio isotopes* ; and (iii) the production of atomic energy by chain reactions due to fission is the subject of *nuclear engineering*.

There are also topics of interest to cosmologists which stem out of nuclear reactions. They are (i) the source of the energy of the sun and the stars and (ii) the age and origin of elements. It is now held that the source of the sun's energy, as well as that of the stars, is in nuclear reactions of a cyclic type in which, according to Bethe, $^{14}_{7}\text{N}$ is a catalyst. The reader is referred to books on Astrophysics for further information. The age of the elements forms the subject of the final chapter of this book.

During this rapid survey of the new knowledge of the nucleus that has been gained during the present century we have seen that a number of elementary particles have been discovered. Before the century opened the electron was the only fundamental particle which had been recognised. In Table 1.1 is listed a number of elementary particles with their charge,

TABLE 1.1

SOME ELEMENTARY PARTICLES

Particle	Symbol	Charge	Approximate Rest-mass		Spin	Stability in Isolation
			Relative	amu		
Neutron	n	0	$1839\ m_e$	1·008937	$\frac{1}{2}$	unstable
Proton	p	$+e$	$1837\ m_e$	1·008130	$\frac{1}{2}$	stable
Negatron	e^-, β^-	$-e$	m_e	0·000584	$\frac{1}{2}$	stable
Positron	e^+, β^+	$+e$	m_e	0·000584	$\frac{1}{2}$	stable
τ-meson	τ	$\pm e$	$1000\ m_e$?	0·600?	?	unstable
π-meson	π	$\pm e$	$293\ m_e$	0·166	?	unstable
μ-meson	μ	$\pm e$	$215\ m_e$	0·126	$\frac{1}{2}$	unstable
ν-meson	ν	0	?	?	?	unstable
Neutrino	ν_o, η	0	0	0	$\frac{1}{2}$	?
Photon	$h\nu, \gamma$	0	0	0	1	stable

approximate rest mass and spin. Particles like α-particles, which are composite, are not included. It is unlikely that the list is complete. Particles of " intermediate mass ", members of the meson family, may yet await discovery. It will be noticed that, so far, no negative proton has been found. The instability of the unstable elementary particles is still under investigation. The half-life of the free neutron is about 20 minutes ; it is a β-emitter. The half lives of the mesons are measured in microseconds.

The Philosophy of Nuclear Physics

We conclude this chapter with a reference to the difficulties of comprehension which face the student of nuclear physics. By this we do not mean the failure to understand at first reading the drift of an intelligible argument, a difficulty which most students experience, but rather an apparent inherent insufficiency of the mental competency of *Homo sapiens* to grasp the inward significance of matters much removed from his normal, immemorial environment. For example, at a time when the quickest mode of travel was, and had been since man attained the stature of man, by horseback, scientists found that the velocity of light was incomparably greater than anything hitherto experienced or imagined. The mathematicians introduced the concept of the four dimensional continuum. So, in 1905, when Einstein introduced both these notions into his relativity theory, there arose a difficulty of comprehension which was a new experience for scientists, a difficulty due not to lack of lucidity in the exposition of a novel theory (that was plentiful !) but to an inherent incapacity of the mind to grasp *pictorially* such strange notions as the conditions for " absolute simultaneity " and a world of four dimensions. Today, the law of gravitation can be considered only in relation to a space-time continuum of four dimensions and the mind is ill equipped, either by nature or by nurture, to enter into the imaginative understanding of this strange world. It is too remote from the three dimensional realm where the imagination naturally constructs its pictures, its models and its animated mechanisms with a facility born of aeons of practice. It is clear, moreover, that such limitations of understanding cannot be removed by lucidity of explanation.

Another familiar illustration of the difficulties of comprehension is found in the wave-particle dualism of light. It is apparently a mental impossibility to form a pictorial conception of the atom or its mechanism of light quantum emission, or of a wave packet *sans* medium. The behaviour of photons in the phenomena of optical interference is to be understood *statistically* ; the path of an individual photon is as unforeseeable as the shape of the photon is inconceivable. There is statistical determinacy, but the causality principal cannot be applied to an individual particle.

Consider, again, an " elementary " particle. Since it cannot be a Euclidean point, it must have extension in space. But this implies structure, which is inconsistent with the elementary nature of the particle. Such considerations have led to the notion that space and time may themselves be quantized ! Heisenburg has suggested that the " smallest length " l_o may be of the order of 10^{-13} cm., and that the " smallest time duration " may be l_o/c. The mind of man, however, is so constituted that it is incapable of accepting the notion of a " smallest length ".

It is clear that we are leaving the arena of the " natural philosopher " and encroaching on the realm of philosophy. The study of the atomic nucleus has certain difficulties which differentiate it in a marked manner from the older studies of classical physics. They are : its incomprehensibility (in the sense explained), its statistical interpretation, with which is associated the failure of the causality principle, and its indeterminacy. May it be that these difficulties are born of the circumstance that man's mental faculties were evolved to allow him to survive in the physical struggle for existence, rather than to enable him to measure the atoms or to weigh the stars?

REFERENCES

C. F. Powell *et al.*, 1946, *Jnl. Sci. Instr.*, 23, 102.
E. Rutherford, 1920, *Bakerian Lecture to the Royal Society*.

CHAPTER II

THE SIZE OF THE NUCLEUS

It was stated in the Introduction to this book that a main *motif* of these pages is a comprehensive survey of the whole family of nuclides from the lightest to the heaviest, having regard to a limited number of their properties such as their mass, their nucleonic composition and their stability. Such a panoramic view will reveal rules and regularities which, in addition to their intrinsic interest, have a direct bearing on the problem of nuclear structure. One of the properties of the nucleus which it is appropriate to include when undertaking a broad survey of the known nuclides is its radius. It is of interest to learn, for example, how the size of the nucleus is related to its mass. It is natural to expect that the heavier nuclei will have the greater volumes, but the question is whether we shall find, as we range from the lowest to the highest atomic numbers, a simple relation between r, the nuclear radius and $_Z^A M$, the nuclear mass, or A, the mass number. We shall find that such a simple relation does exist. It is one of the fundamental facts of nuclear physics.

Early Methods of Measurement

There are four principal methods of measuring the radius of the nucleus. They have nothing in common except that they lead to the same results. The first estimates of the nuclear size to be based on careful measurements were made by Rutherford, who was himself the author of the concept of the nuclear atom. Before 1910 the view of atomic structure which was most widely held was that it was a distribution of " negative corpuscles " (electrons) embedded in a sphere of diffuse positive electricity, the whole being electrically neutral. Rutherford and his associates, in a series of classic experiments, bombarded thin metal foil with α-particles which in their passage through the foil, were deflected through measured angles (Fig. 2.1). Assuming that the nuclear charge, Ze, was concentrated at a point and

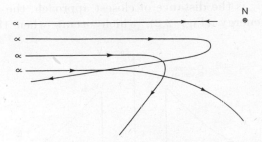

FIG. 2.1. Scattering of α-particles by a nucleus (N).

that the incident α-particle was also a point charge moving with velocity v, Rutherford established the formula

$$f(\theta) = \left(\frac{Ze^2}{\bar{M}v^2}\right)^2 \operatorname{cosec}^4 \frac{\theta}{2} \qquad (2.1)$$

where θ is the angle of scattering in the common C. of G. coordinate system and $\bar{M}$ is the reduced mass of the incident α-particle. Rutherford confirmed that Eq. (2.1) held for the mono-energetic α-particles emitted by certain radioactive elements except when the particles made almost head-on collisions with the nucleus. In such cases there was, for light nuclei, a deviation from the classical scattering formula. The deviations were not observed in the case of the heavy nuclei. This anomalous scattering, corresponding to a close approach of the α-particle to the nucleus, was attributed to some short-range *attractive* forces differing in nature from the Coulomb inverse square law forces. The distance from the nucleus centre at which these attractive forces become appreciable is assumed to be the radius of the nucleus.

The graph of *potential v. nuclear distance* is qualitatively represented in Fig. 2.2 where r_0 is approximately the radius of a nucleus having its centre at the origin of co-ordinates.

An approximate estimate of the size of an atomic nucleus may be made by a simple calculation. Consider an α-particle, of mass m and charge $2e$ moving with velocity v, which is turned back along its own path in making a head-on collision with a nucleus of charge Ze. By Coulomb's law the repulsive force between the particles is $2Ze^2/r^2$, where r is the distance between them. If r_0 is the distance of closest approach, the maximum potential energy (Fig. 2.2), which occurs when the kinetic

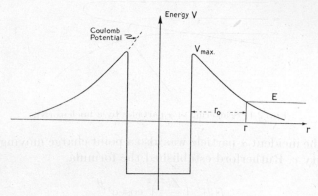

FIG. 2.2. The " potential well ".

energy is zero, is $2Ze^2/r_0$. Since the total energy is constant,

$$2Ze^2/r_0 = \tfrac{1}{2}mv^2 \qquad (2.2)$$

whence $$r_0 = 4Ze^2/mv^2 \qquad (2.3)$$

$e = 4 \cdot 8 \times 10^{-10}$ e.s.u., $m = 6 \cdot 65 \times 10^{-24}$ gm. and v is about $1 \cdot 5 \times 10^9$ cm. sec^{-1}. If we take Z to be 16 (sulphur), r_0 is found to be approximately 10^{-12} cm. so that the radius of the sulphur nucleus must be less than 10^{-12} cm.

The scattering experiments of Chadwick, Geiger and Marsden showed that the inverse square law held to distances of 10^{-11} cm., so that the diameter of the nucleus could not be much greater than 10^{-12} cm. Other experiments in Rutherford's laboratory showed that α-particles having a velocity of $1 \cdot 4 \times 10^9$ cm. sec.$^{-1}$ can reach a point within 5×10^{-13} cm. of a hydrogen nucleus without violation of the Coulomb law of repulsion.

Rutherford-Bohr Atom

Niels Bohr linked the Rutherford model of the atom quantitatively to the quantum theory and was able to obtain a theoretical derivation of the well-known relation between the frequencies of the lines of the hydrogen spectrum. To-day, the Rutherford-Bohr model is firmly established in its essential features. The results of the remarkable series of experiments referred to above could be explained on the hypothesis that the mass of the atom, so far from being diffuse, is almost entirely concentrated into an extremely small volume, the " nucleus ", which is positively charged. Surrounding this central core are particles of negative electricity which, while neutralizing completely the positive charge of the nucleus, account for only one part in several thousands of its mass. Rutherford's experiments not only established the nuclear model of the atom but also arranged the elements in a definite order specified by their *atomic number, Z.* For the first twenty elements Z was about half the integer nearest to the atomic weight and less than half for elements of higher atomic number. Moreover, it was found that the arrangement of the elements in order of their ascending atomic number was significant. Not only did this order practically coincide with that of the chemist's periodic table but it had meanings for the physicist which it is a main purpose of these pages to discuss.

Later Methods of Measurement

Since the time of these historic and fundamental experiments three other principal methods of determining nuclear radii have been developed. One of these, based on the quantum-mechanical theory of alpha radioactivity, is concerned only with the heaviest elements $(Z > 82)$. Another depends on the determination of the cross-sections of nuclei with respect to fast neutrons and to charged particles producing nuclear reactions. The third is based on the effect which the electrostatic interaction of protons in the nucleus has on its binding energy. These methods of estimating the size of the nucleus will now be described. The close agreement between the results of four methods which differ so widely in principle affords satisfactory confirmation both of the hypothesis of the nuclear atom and of the size attributed to the nucleus.

I. *Half-lives of elements emitting α-particles*

It has been one of the achievements of quantum mechanics to relate the half-life of a radioactive element to the energy of the emitted α-particle and also to the radius of the nucleus. The range of values of the half-lives is enormous as the following comparison shows :

Element	Energy of α-particle	Half-life
Radium C′	7·83 MeV.	$1·5 \times 10^{-4}$ sec.
Thorium	4·34 MeV.	2×10^{10} years

In view of such wide variations the consistency of the calculated radii of the heavy nuclei based on these figures is remarkable.

The quantum mechanical theory of alpha radioactivity originated in an attempt to account for a simple empirical relationship between the half-life of an alpha emitter and the energy of the emitted particle. The theory required the radius r_0 of the nucleus to be one of the parameters, so that it afforded a method of estimating the size of the nucleus. Full accounts of the theory may be found in text-books devoted to nuclear theory. Here only a brief outline of the argument will be given.

In 1907 Rutherford suggested that there might be a connection between the energy of an emitted α-particle and the half-life of the parent element. In 1911 this empirical rule was discovered by H. Geiger and J. M. Nuttall, who showed that a plot of the logarithm of its decay constant λ *versus* log range R in air of the α-particle was approximately a straight line. The *Geiger-Nuttall rule* is therefore expressed by the equation

$$\log \lambda = A \log R + B \qquad (2.4)$$

where A is a constant for all four radioactive series and B is a constant having values which are different for the different series.

The decay constant λ is related to the half-life τ by the relation $\tau = 0·693/\lambda$, and the range R is related to the initial energy E of the ejected α-particle by the equation $E \simeq \text{const.} R$. The Geiger-Nuttall rule may therefore be expressed by the equation

$$-\log \tau = A_1 \log E + B_1 \qquad (2.5)$$

This form of the rule is shown graphically for the uranium—or $(4n + 2)$—series in Fig. 2.3. The $(4n)$, $(4n + 1)$ and $(4n + 2)$ series are represented by similar diagrams. Although the graphs indicate departures from a strictly linear relation between $\log \tau$ and $\log E$, it is clear that high energies are associated with short half-lives, and conversely, over a very wide range of values of τ.

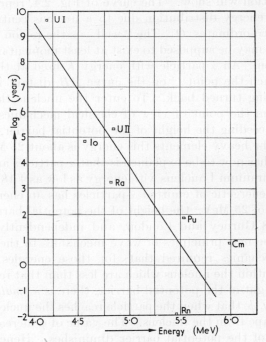

FIG. 2.3. The (4n + 2) radioactive series : log E v. log τ

The theoretical explanation of the Geiger-Nuttall rule was an achievement of quantum mechanics. It proved to be inexplicable on the basis of classical mechanics, as the following

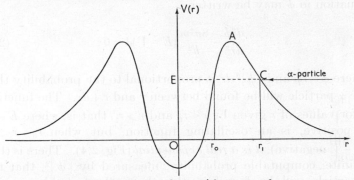

FIG. 2.4. Incidence of α-particle on a nucleus.

consideration will show. The curve of Fig. 2.4, represents the potential energy distribution due to a nucleus centred at the origin of co-ordinates, O. The " well " is the region where the α-particle may be supposed to exist at least momentarily before its ejection. An α-particle with energy E fired at the nucleus would reach the point C on the curve AB, distant r_1 from O, before being turned back. To enter the nucleus the particle must, from the point of view of classical mechanics, have an energy exceeding the height of the potential barrier, the point A. For the heavy elements this energy is about 25 MeV. The fact that has now to be explained is that α-particles are emitted from the uranium I nucleus with energy as low as 4·18 MeV. and the most energetic of emitted α-particles has an energy of less than half of 25 MeV., the height of the potential barrier.

In 1928 Gurney and Condon, and independently Gamow, applied the new principles of wave mechanics to the problem. Wave mechanics required that, for those energies of an α-particle within the nucleus which are less than that represented by the height of the potential barrier, there is a *small but finite probability*, ϕ, that when the particle reaches the nuclear surface it will escape from the nucleus. The value of ϕ increases as the thickness of the potential barrier diminishes. Hence, as Fig. 2.4 shows, the probability of escape is greater the larger the energy of the α-particle. Since a high probability of α-emission means a short half-life, this points to an explanation of the Geiger-Nuttall rule.

The wave mechanics theory shows that the Schroedinger equation in ϕ may be written

$$\frac{d^2\phi}{dr^2} + \frac{8\pi^2 m}{h^2}(E - V)\phi = 0 \tag{2.6}$$

where $\phi = r\psi$ and $|\phi|^2\,dr$ is proportional to the probability that the α-particle will be found between r and $\overline{r + dr}$. The function ϕ for values of r given by $r < r_0$ and $r > r_1$, that is, where $\overline{E - V}$ is positive, is an oscillating function, but when $r_0 < r < r_1$, $(\overline{E - V}$ negative$)$, *it is a real exponential* (Fig. 2.4). There is thus a finite, computable probability, measured by $|\phi|^2$, that the α-particle will be found in the classically forbidden region denoted by $r_0 < r < r_1$. It may be shown by the method of wave mechanics that the solution of (2.6) is

$$\phi = k \exp. \left[-\frac{4\pi\sqrt{2m}}{h} \int_{r_0}^{r_1} (V - E) \, dr \right] \qquad (2.7)$$

where V is the Coulomb potential energy $2Ze^2/r$, E is the disintegration energy and m is the mass of the α-particle. This expression is sometimes called the *transmission coefficient* of the potential barrier.

The full theory is found in the literature of the subject (e.g. Gamow and Critchfield, 1950). It must suffice here to point out that Eq. (2.7) leads to the Geiger-Nuttall rule. It will be seen from this equation, as well as from Fig. 2.4, that low values of the energy E of the emitted α-particle correspond to low values of the probability of emission, and hence to long half-lives, and conversely, as the Geiger-Nuttall rule requires. It is, however, more important for our present purpose to notice that the half-life of a heavy radio-element, a quantity which can be accurately measured, is connected through ϕ in Eq. (2.7) to the radius r_0* of the nucleus. This connection is obtained by evaluation of the integral. It may be illustrated by a crude, semi-classical illustration.

Let it be assumed that the average speed of an α-particle moving along a diameter within a thorium nucleus is 10^9 cm. sec^{-1}. The particle reaches the nuclear surface with a frequency of $10^9/2r_0$ per second. While it is at the surface there is a finite probability of escape, ϕ, given by wave-mechanical theory. The product of ϕ and the frequency $10^9/2r_0$ is the decay constant λ :

$$\phi \times 10^9/2r_0 = \lambda \qquad (2.8)$$

The value of λ for thorium is about 10^{-18} sec^{-1}. The value of ϕ must be calculated from Eq. (2.7). Taking it as 10^{-39} we obtain

$$r_0 = 5 \times 10^{-13} \text{ cm}. \qquad (2.9)$$

The calculated values of the nuclear radii for the radioactive elements vary from 0.6 to 0.9 $\times 10^{-12}$ cm. The values of the radii r for members of the uranium series are given in Table 2.1.

* This r is not the same as that on p. 22.

TABLE 2.1

Nuclide	Z	A	$r \times 10^{13}$ cm.	$r_0 \times 10^{13}$ cm.
Pu	94	238	9·2	1·49
UII	92	234	9·2	1·49
Io	90	230	8·5	1·39
Ra	88	226	8·1	1·33
Rn	86	222	7·9	1·31
RaA	84	218	7·7	1·28

The Table 2.1 is expressed graphically in Fig. 2.5.

It will be seen that for heavy nuclei the radius increases with the mass number. The simplest relation commonly given

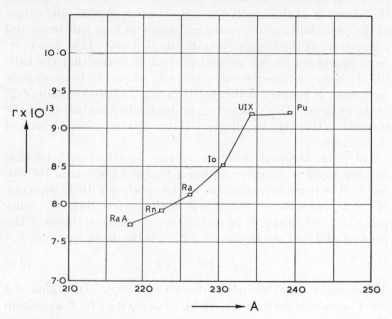

FIG. 2.5. Nuclear radii of some α-emitters as a function of atomic mass number.

between these two quantities and one which is sufficiently accurate for many practical applications is

$$r = r_0 \times A^{\frac{1}{3}} \qquad (2.10)$$

where r_0 is, for a wide range of values of A, approximately constant. From the calculated values of r_0 shown in Table 2.1, it is evident that the connection between r and A is not quite as simple as that expressed in Eq. (2.10) for the heaviest elements. The appropriate comment, however, on Table 2.1 is not that it shows a deviation from Eq. (2.10), but rather that, having regard to the indirect method of evaluating r, involving abstruse theoretical arguments, the values of r agree closely with those to be expected from the hypothesis of constancy of nuclear density as expressed in Eq. (2.10).

II. *Cross-sections of Nuclei*

When a collimated beam of elementary particles or photons impinges normally on a material surface, there is a finite probability of either scattering, absorption or nuclear reaction. This probability is expressed as a *cross-section*, σ. An imaginary circular disc is assumed to be centred on each nucleus with its plane normal to the incident beam. It has an area such that, if an incident particle passes through it, interaction takes place ; if it passes outside the disc, there is no interaction. Cross-sections are measured in sq. cm. or in *barns* : 1 barn $= 10^{-24}$ cm.^{2} Clearly, the values of σ will vary widely according to the great variety of factors affecting the interactions. A few examples will illustrate this. The probability that a photon of 2.6 MeV. energy will disintegrate a deuteron is expressed by $\sigma = 1\cdot2 \times 10^{-3}$ bn. ($= 1\cdot2 \times 10^{-27}$ cm.^{2}) for this reaction. In this case, therefore, the imaginary disc is but little larger than the nuclear cross-section. By contrast, if boron is bombarded by thermal neutrons, the *capture cross-section* is 1600 bn. The disc diameter in this case is therefore many times larger than the diameter of the nucleus, being about 460×10^{-13} cm. For neutrons of higher velocity, 10^6 cm. sec.$^{-1}$, $\sigma = 160$ bn. only. From this example it is to be expected that, as the neutron velocity increases, the extrapolated value of σ will approach the cross-sectional area of the nucleus. The neutron wave-length $\lambda/2\pi$ (*v.* p. 38) must be small compared with the nuclear diameter.

The measurement of the cross-sections of nuclei bombarded with fast neutrons affords the most general and the most direct experimental method of determining nuclear radii. The

D   H.N.S.

reduction in the intensity of a beam of fast monochromatic neutrons, which results from the passage of the neutrons through a known thickness of the substance under investigation, is a measure of σ, since each nucleus presents a cross-section of $\pi d^2/4$ to a fast neutron. Measurements covering a wide range of nuclear masses (Fernbach et al., 1949 ; Feshbach et al., 1949 ; Cook et al., 1949), in which a homogeneous beam of very fast neutrons was used, produced a linear relation of remarkable accuracy between the volume and the mass number of the nucleus. This relation is expressed by the Eq. (2.10). The most generally useful value of r_0 appears to be 1.39×10^{-13}. This noteworthy equation, which is expressed graphically in Fig. 2.6 applies to light, medium-weight and heavy nuclei. The experiments from which it is derived accordingly support

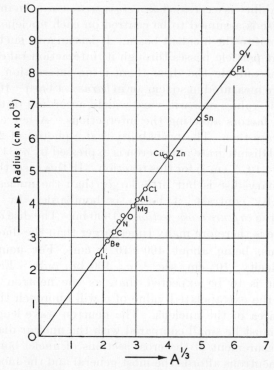

Fig. 2.6. Nuclear radii deduced from total cross section $v.$ $A^{\frac{1}{3}}$.

the hypothesis of the constancy of the density of nuclear matter.

Later experiments undertaken at Berkeley (Hildebrand and Leith, 1950) with 33 nuclides, using neutrons of 42 MeV., have suggested that, as we pass from the lightest to the heaviest nuclei, there is a process of *shell formation* similar to that well known in connection with the circumnuclear electrons, and that the radii of the nuclei depend to a small but measureable extent on the stage reached in the formation of completed shells (D. Curie, 1951).

The nuclear radii increase steadily with increasing mass number according to the equation

$$r = r_0 A^{\frac{1}{3}} + b \qquad (2.11)$$

where r_0 and b are constants which suffer sudden small changes of value when $Z = 8$, 20, 50 and 82. These numbers, called " the magic numbers " (Chap. X), are associated with the completion of nuclear shells. According to D. Curie (1951) the following values of nuclear radii fit the results of the most recent experiments for measuring cross-sections for very fast neutrons :

$$\left.\begin{array}{ll}
{}_3\text{Li to }{}_8\text{O} & r = 2 \cdot 34 A^{\frac{1}{3}} - 1 \cdot 96 \\[4pt]
{}_8\text{O to }{}_{20}\text{Ca} & r = 1 \cdot 26 A^{\frac{1}{3}} + 0 \cdot 88 \\[4pt]
{}_{26}\text{Fe to }{}_{50}\text{Sn} & r = 0 \cdot 98 A^{\frac{1}{3}} + 1 \cdot 79 \\[4pt]
{}_{50}\text{Sn to }{}_{92}\text{U} & r = 1 \cdot 37 A^{\frac{1}{3}} + 1 \cdot 30
\end{array}\right\} \times 10^{-13} \text{ cm.} \qquad (2.12)$$

The graph of Fig. 2.7, representing these equations, shows a number of " kinks " corresponding with the completion of nuclear shells, that is, with nuclei of unusual stability. The reader should note that the values of r_0 and b given above are provisional and subject to modification in the light of further study.

The method of measuring the size of nuclei by determining their cross-sections in respect of irradiation by fast neutrons is not only the most general method, applying to the whole range of nuclides, but it promises to become, as technical methods improve, the most reliable and accurate. It appears to be established by this method that the nuclear radius can be expressed with considerable accuracy by Eq. (2.11), a result of great importance.

Reactions of nuclei with incident charged particles involve the penetration of the spherical potential barrier enveloping the

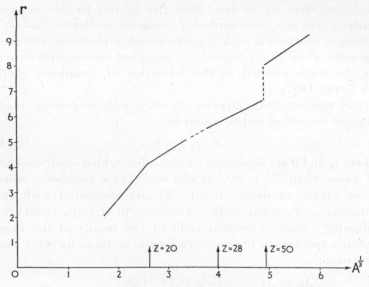

FIG. 2.7. Graph of Eq. (2.12) suggesting " magic numbers ".

nucleus. By comparing the cross-sections for such reactions with the fast neutron cross-sections the " transmission " of the barrier is obtained. From this, by methods similar to those used for α-particle emission from the radioactive nuclei, the radii of stable nuclei may be calculated. Eq. (2.10) is found to hold also for these cases.

III. *Binding Energies of Mirror Nuclides*

If a pair of nuclides is so constituted that either can be transformed into the other by changing proton into neutron and neutron into proton, they are called *mirror nuclides*. An example is :

$^{15}_{7}N$ having 7 protons and 8 neutrons.
$^{15}_{8}O$ having 8 protons and 7 neutrons.

Examples are listed in Table 2.2.

TABLE 2.2

MIRROR NUCLIDES

$^{3}_{1}H$	$^{3}_{2}He$
$^{7}_{3}Li$	$^{7}_{4}Be$
$^{11}_{5}B$	$^{11}_{6}C$
$^{13}_{6}C$	$^{13}_{7}N$
$^{15}_{7}N$	$^{15}_{8}O$
$^{29}_{14}Si$	$^{29}_{15}P$

If the difference in binding energy between members of a pair is known, the radii of their nuclei may be calculated on the assumption that the whole difference of energy is due to Coulomb repulsion. This means that the p-p and n-n nuclear interactions are assumed to be equal.

Mirror nuclides are isobars. In this section those mirror nuclides are considered in which the number of protons differs from the number of neutrons by one, that is, *adjacent isobars* having isotopic numbers $+1$ and -1. It is known that, with three doubtful exceptions, in all such isobaric pairs one member is unstable against beta decay. For example, $^{15}_{8}O$ is unstable against positron decay :

$$^{15}_{8}O \rightarrow {}^{15}_{7}N + \beta^{+}$$

We shall now derive an expression by which the radius of a mirror nuclide may be related to a measurement of binding energies. It is based, as we have said, on the assumption that the whole difference of binding energies is due to the electrostatic repulsion between the protons of the nucleus.

Let $^{A-1}_{Z}M$ be the mass of a nucleus (e.g. $^{14}_{7}N$). The addition of a neutron to form a nucleus of mass $^{A}_{Z}M$ produces an increase of mass equal to the mass of the neutron m_n, less B_n, the binding energy of this particle. We have, therefore, the energy balance :

$$(^{A-1}_{Z}M + m_n)c^2 - B_n = {}^{A}_{Z}Mc^2 \tag{2.13}$$

(In this equation, if the masses are in grams, the energy is in ergs).

If electrostatic repulsion is neglected, a parallel equation stands for an added proton :

$$(^{A}_{Z}M + m_p)c^2 - B_p = _{Z+1}^{A}Mc^2$$

TABLE 2.3

		Period	Z	$\dfrac{(M_{z+1} - M_z)c^2}{\text{mmu}}$	$\dfrac{r}{10^{-13}\text{ cm}}$	$\dfrac{r_0}{10^{-13}\text{ cm}}$
^{11}C	^{11}B	20·5 min	5	2·11	3·19	1·43
^{13}N	^{13}C	10·1 min	6	2·11	3·83	1·63
^{15}O	^{15}N	126 sec	7	2·91	3·50	1·42
^{17}F	^{17}O	70 sec	8	3·0	3·91	1·52
^{19}Ne	^{19}F	20·3 sec	9	3·31	4·07	1·53
^{21}Na	^{21}Ne	23 sec	10	3·9	3·96	1·44
^{23}Mg	^{23}Na	11·6 sec	11	4·0	4·26	1·50
^{25}Al	^{25}Mg	7·3 sec	12	4·3	4·38	1·50
^{27}Si	^{27}Al	4·9 sec	13	5·0	4·17	1·39
^{29}P	^{29}Si	4·6 sec	14	5·3	4·27	1·39
^{31}S	^{31}P	3·2 sec	15	5·6	4·36	1·39
^{33}Cl	^{33}S	2·4 sec	16	6·0	4·38	1·37
^{35}A	^{35}Cl	1·88 sec	17	6·3	4·45	1·36
^{39}Ca	^{39}K	1·06 sec	19	?	—	—
^{41}Sc	^{41}Ca	0·87 sec	20	6·4	4·80	1·42

But the proton has in fact diminished the binding energy B_p of the nucleus by the Coulomb energy. As is proved in Appendix II this is $6Ze^2/5r$, so that the last equation must be amended to

$$(^{A}_{Z}M + m_p)c^2 - \left(B_p - \frac{6e^2}{5r}Z\right) = _{Z+1}^{A}Mc^2. \qquad (2.14)$$

From (2.13) and (2.14) we obtain

$$(_{Z+1}^{A}M - ^{A}_{Z}M)c^2 = (m_p - m_n)c^2 + (B_n - B_p) + \frac{6e^2}{5r}Z. \qquad (2.15)$$

We now assume that $(B_n - B_p)$ is negligibly small in comparison with the last term and obtain after re-arrangement :

$$r = \frac{6e^2Z}{5c^2} \cdot \frac{1}{(_{Z+1}^{A}M - ^{A}_{Z}M) + (m_n - m_p)} . \qquad (2.16)$$

Table 2.3 shows some radii calculated from this equation. The variation of r with $A^{\frac{1}{3}}$ is shown in Fig. 2.8. The close agreement between the values of r found by this method and

those found by other methods supports the assumption that the
nuclear p-p and n-n forces are nearly equal.

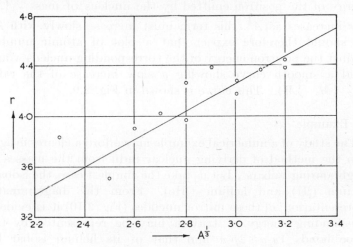

FIG. 2.8. Graph of Table 2.3.

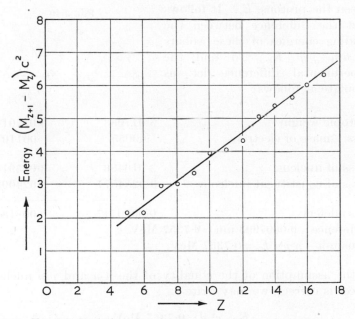

FIG. 2.9. Variation of positron energy with atomic number.

The result given by Eq. (2.16) may be expressed in another way. The denominator term $(_{Z+1}^{A}M - _{Z}^{A}M)c^2$ is the maximum energy of the positron emitted by the nucleus of mass $_{Z+1}^{A}M$. If r increases as $A^{\frac{1}{3}}$, this term must increase slowly with Z; we should therefore expect that a plot of atomic number against the positron energy of the corresponding nucleus would yield a smooth curve showing a slow increase of the ratio $Z/(_{Z+1}^{A}M - _{Z}^{A}M)$. This curve is shown in Fig. 2.9.

An Example

The study of a numerical example may afford a clearer insight into the method of deriving nuclear radii from the masses of neighbouring isobars. Let us take the simplest case, the isobars tritium ($_{1}^{3}$H) and helium ($_{2}^{3}$He). From the diagrammatic representation of these mirror nuclides (Fig. 2.10) it is evident the binding energy of tritium may be represented by the three bonds $1n\text{-}n + 2p\text{-}n$ and that of its helium isobar by the three bonds $1p\text{-}p + 2p\text{-}n$ *less* the Coulomb energy between the protons, E_c. It follows that the difference between the binding energies of these isobars is $n\text{-}n - p\text{-}p + E_c$. To find the experimental difference let us tabulate as follows:

FIG. 2-10

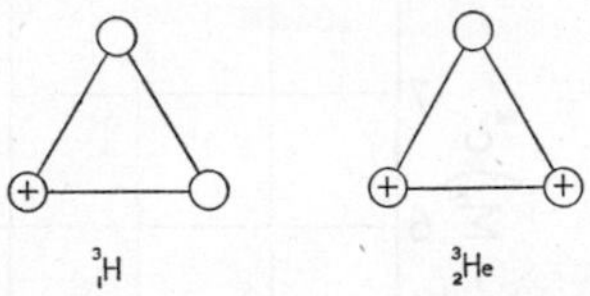

	$_{1}^{3}$H	$_{2}^{3}$He
Isotopic weight	3·017033	3·017014
Less : mass of electrons	·00055	·00110
Mass of nucleus	3·016483	3·015914
Mass of constituent nucleons	3·0254577	3·0240984
Mass defect	0·0089747	0·0081844

Difference $= 0\cdot0007903$ mu $= 0\cdot7357$ MeV.
Thus $n\text{-}n - p\text{-}p + E_c = 0\cdot7357$ MeV.

If the assumption of the equality of the $n\text{-}n$ and $p\text{-}p$ nuclear forces is correct, we may write

$$E_c = e^2/d = 0\cdot7357 \text{ MeV.}$$

where e is the charge on each of the protons ($4 \cdot 77 \times 10^{-10}$ e.s.u.) and d is their distance apart. From this equation we find

$$d = 1 \cdot 96 \times 10^{-13} \text{ cm.}$$

Taking r as $d \cdot \sqrt{3}/3$, we obtain

$$r = 1 \cdot 13 \times 10^{13} \text{ cm.}$$

The argument, though somewhat crude and oversimplified, nevertheless produces a result of the right order.

Density of Nuclear Matter

The several independent lines of enquiry into the size of the nucleus described in this Chapter yield remarkably consistent results and lead to the important conclusion that the radius of the nucleus may be represented by the equation

$$r = r_0 \cdot A^{\frac{1}{3}} + b \qquad (2.11)$$

For many purposes we may take the value of b to be zero and the value of r_0 to vary from $1 \cdot 30 \times 10^{-13}$ cm. for light nuclei to $1 \cdot 48 \times 10^{-13}$ cm. for heavy nuclei. Taking a mean value we may therefore write

$$r = 1 \cdot 39 \times 10^{-13} A^{\frac{1}{3}} \text{ cm.} \qquad (2.17)$$

It is clear from this that the nucleus is much smaller than the atom. This is to be expected from the complete identity of the chemical and physical properties of the isotopes of an element. If the diameter of the nucleus or of any field of force originating in it were comparable with that of the atom, it would be reasonable to expect differences in the properties of the isotopes of a given element. These differences, however, except in respect of the Coulomb forces, are notably absent.

Since the mass number A corresponds closely to the mass of the nucleus, it follows from Eq. (2.17) that the density of all nuclei is approximately the same. In other words, the volume occupied by a nucleon is constant for all nuclei. Taking the mass of a nucleon as $1 \cdot 7 \times 10^{-24}$ gm., we find the density of nuclear matter to be about 150,000 tons per cubic millimetre!

The density of the type of star known as the White Dwarf, while not approaching this value, is much higher than anything known on earth. It is established that for some White Dwarfs the density of the matter for which they are composed is several million times that of water. This must mean that the atoms of such a star are packed very tightly together, and the nuclei, though still relatively widely separated, are much closer than they are in matter existing in the great majority of stars.

The constancy of density of nuclear matter is in sharp contrast with the wide range of values in the densities of the elements. It is comparable in this respect with the density of the drops of a liquid which is independent of their radii. We shall see that this analogy between a liquid drop and an atomic nucleus has proved suggestive.

Size and Shape of the Nucleus

The " emptiness " of the atom is evident from a comparison of atomic with nuclear volumes. The radius of the atom of argon (^{40}A), for example, is about $1 \cdot 5 \times 10^{-8}$ cm., while the nucleus has a radius of approximately 5×10^{-13} cm.

The ratio of the volumes is therefore about 10^{14}. To assist the imagination it may be remarked that the size of a cathedral would bear about the same ratio to the size of a house-fly! It is therefore not difficult to understand that uncharged particles of nuclear dimensions can pass easily through a considerable thickness of matter.

The experimentally determined value of the radius of the nucleus supports the view that nuclei are formed of neutrons and protons (nucleons) rather than of protons and electrons as was at one time supposed. For the de Broglie wave-length of a nucleon of kinetic energy 8 MeV., a value which is of the same order as the binding energy of a nucleon, is

$$\lambda/2\pi = h/2\pi\sqrt{ME} = 1 \cdot 5 \times 10^{-13} \text{ cm.}$$

But for electrons at this relativistic energy the value of $\lambda/2\pi$ would be about $2 \cdot 5 \times 10^{-12}$ cm. This is much greater than the diameter of the largest nucleus, whereas the wave-length of a nucleon of appropriate energy is of the right order of magnitude.

It has been assumed that the shape of a nucleus is spherical. For light nuclei this is a sufficient approximation. There are, however, reasons for believing that the approximation is not so good for heavy nuclei. Recently, results obtained by the method of microwave spectroscopy have suggested that there is a deviation from spherical symmetry and that a prolate or oblate spheroid is a closer approximation. The difference is small, amounting to a prolongation or shortening of the spin axis of the order of about one per cent. In the case of the heaviest nuclei, which tend by the process of fission to split into two parts, the asymmetry is more marked.

Since it is the aim in these pages to view the whole family of isotopes rather than to consider individual species, the primary interest lies in observing how certain parameters vary as the survey of the nuclides ranges from the lightest to the heaviest. This panoramic view has revealed certain facts of importance, such as the smooth increase of nuclear volume between the limits $Z = 1$ and $Z = 92$, the constancy of the density of nuclear matter and the near-equality of the p-p and n-n forces.

We sum up these results as follows :

1. *The radius of any nucleus, assumed spherical, may be expressed by the formula :*

$$r = r_0 \times 10^{-13} A^{\frac{1}{3}} \text{ cm.}$$

In this equation the value of r_0 varies from 1·30 to 1·48.

2. *The density of nuclear matter is constant.* The value is approximately 10^{14} gm. per c.c.

3. *The nuclear forces p-p and n-n are approximately equal.* Nuclear forces are saturated (*v.* p. 141). The Coulomb force between protons, however, is not saturated. It becomes the predominant influence in the case of the heaviest nuclei and is associated with nuclear fission and radioactivity.

REFERENCES

Cook, Macmillan, Petersen and Sewell, 1948, *Phys. Rev.*, 75, 7.

D. Curie, 1951, *Jnl. de Phys. et le Rad.*, 12, 570.

S. Fernbach, R. Serber and T. B. Taylor, 1949, *Phys. Rev.*, 75, 1352.

Feshbach and Weisskopf, 1949, *Phys. Rev.*, 76, 1550.

G. Gamow and C. L. Critchfield, 1950, *Theory of Atomic Nucleus and Nuclear Energy Sources*, Chap. VI.

R. H. Hildebrand and C. E. Leith, 1950, *Phys. Rev.*, 80, 843.

CHAPTER III

ISOTOPES

Isotopy was discovered in 1906 : it was one of the results of the study of natural radioactivity. A new radioactive element, named by its discoverer *ionium* (Boltwood, 1906) was found to have chemical properties indistinguishable from those of thorium. The spectra of the two elements were identical and it was shown that the only observable differences between them were in respect of their radioactive properties and their atomic weights. Their equal claim to occupy the same place in the chemist's periodic classification of the elements gave their species its name. Elements having identical chemical properties but differing atomic masses were named by the English chemist Soddy *isotopes*, from the Greek ισος (equal) τοπος (place). In 1914 the discovery was made that isotopes existed among the non-radioactive elements. Honigschmid showed that the lead which was the end product of the thorium radioactive series had an atomic weight of 207.90, whereas the lead which was the final result of the decay of the uranium series had an atomic weight of 206·05. At about the same time, J. J. Thomson discovered, while investigating positive rays, that the noble gas neon consisted of a mixture of three species of atoms differentiated only by their having different masses. In the years following the first world war Aston, developing the positive ray tube into a sensitive instrument which he called a *mass spectrograph*, showed that the majority of the element were mixtures of isotopes.

The present chapter will be chiefly concerned with a description of the methods by which the existence of the isotopes has been demonstrated and their relative abundance and masses, on the scale $^{16}O = 16$, determined. The measurements have established the important result that, relative to $^{16}O = 16$, the masses of isotopes differ from integral numbers by less than one per cent, in harmony with the current hypothesis that nuclei are formed of protons and neutrons.

Four methods have been employed to identify the isotopes of an element. In the chronological order of their development they are :

1. By the study of natural radioactivity.
2. By means of the mass spectrograph.
3. By measurements of the energy balance of nuclear reactions.
4. By investigations of the hyperfine structure of spectral lines.

Of these it may be said that the first is mainly of historical interest, the second has proved to be by far the most fruitful to date, the third is of limited application but provides useful corroborative evidence, and the fourth is a new development.

I. *The Mass Spectrograph*

The instrument which has been the means of discovering most of the facts relating to nuclear mass is the *mass spectrograph*. A variety of types have been developed, each adapted to a special purpose but all having the common aim of determining the mass of an isotope with as high a degree of accuracy as possible. Since nuclear mass is a main topic of this book and the mass spectrograph is the key instrument for measuring nuclear mass, space is devoted to discussing the origin, the function and the various types of this apparatus.

The classical method of studying isotopes originated in 1912 in the investigation of *positive rays* by W. Wien and J. J. Thomson. Thomson subjected a narrow, collimated beam of positively charged ions—the " positive rays "—to parallel, superimposed electrostatic and magnetic fields. The simple theory of the experiment may be briefly stated.

Suppose that a positively charged particle of mass m and charge e is travelling with velocity v towards O (Fig. 3.1) in a direction normal to the paper. Then it can be shown (Starling, 1946) that a uniform electric field E parallel to the Ox axis will cause the particle to strike the paper at a point $(x, 0)$ where

$$x = k_1 \frac{Ee}{mv^2}. \tag{3.1}$$

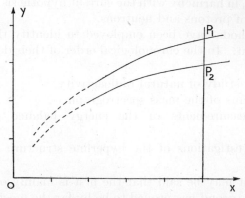

FIG. 3.1. Parabolas produced by positive rays.

If a magnetic field parallel to the $0x$ axis is substituted for the electric field, the particle will strike the paper at a point $(0, y)$ where

$$y = k_2 \frac{He}{mv}. \tag{3.2}$$

If these electric and magnetic fields are applied simultaneously, the particle will strike the paper at a point (x, y)—P_1, Fig. 3.1—which is found by eliminating v from (3.1) and (3.2) :

$$x = k \cdot \frac{E}{H^2} \cdot \frac{m}{e} \cdot y^2. \tag{3.3}$$

Consider a stream of particles for which the ratio m/e is the same for all. If E/H^2 is maintained at a constant value, particles of different velocities will strike the paper at points which lie on the parabola.

$$x = \text{constant} \times y^2 \tag{3.4}$$

If particles having a different value of m/e move through the fields, a different parabola, OP_2, will be recorded. Finally, if the charges of ions of different mass, m_1 and m_2, are equal, then the ordinates y_1 and y_2 of the two parabolas for the same value of the abscissa x are, from Eq. (3.3), related by the equation :

$$\frac{y_1^2}{y_2^2} = \frac{m_2/e}{m_1/e}$$

Fig. 3. 2(*a*)   Aston's mass spectrograph, Cavendish laboratory, 1919.

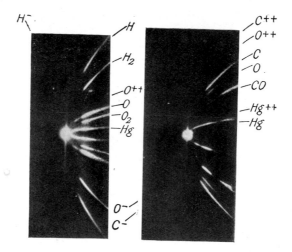

FIG. 3. 2(*b*)   Original and typical positive ray parabolas (1911).
From Aston *Mass Spectra and Isotopes* (Arnold)

that is,

$$\frac{m_1}{m_2} = \left(\frac{y_2}{y_1}\right)^2. \tag{3.5}$$

Hence the masses of the two ions of equal charge may be compared by measuring the ratio y_1/y_2.

The parabolas shown in Fig. 3.2 are typical of results obtained by Thomson when the positive rays were allowed to fall on a photographic plate. The additional parabolas seen in the Figure result from reversing the direction of either the electric or the magnetic field. In his book *Rays of Positive Electricity* (1913), Thomson was cautious. Referring to the similarity of the optical spectra of enriched neon (20) and neon (22) he writes: " . . . this gives some grounds for the suspicion that the two gases, although of different atomic weights, may be indistinguishable in their chemical and spectroscopic properties ". The " suspicion " was fully confirmed. Neon was later shown conclusively to exist in three isotopic forms with atomic masses 20, 21, and 22.

Following Thomson's classic experiments a number of similar instruments differing somewhat in functional aims were constructed. Some of these employed a photographic plate for recording mass values ; they were called mass spectrographs. Others used an electrical method to measure the density of the ion stream ; these were named mass spectrometers. Some instruments, such as Nier's, were designed to use gases as the source of the ion stream ; others worked with samples in the solid form. Different types covered different ranges of atomic masses. Some yielded a very accurate mass difference between nuclei of almost equal mass (doublets, p. 49), others determined the relative abundance of the isotopes of a given element.

The pioneer, after Thomson, in mass spectrographic investigations, the results of which have so greatly augmented our knowledge of the elements and of the nucleus of the atom, was his colleague, F. W. Aston. His original apparatus and methods have been refined and improved by a number of workers, including Dempster, Bainbridge, Jordan, Nier and Mattauch.

Aston's first mass spectrograph was not capable of measuring

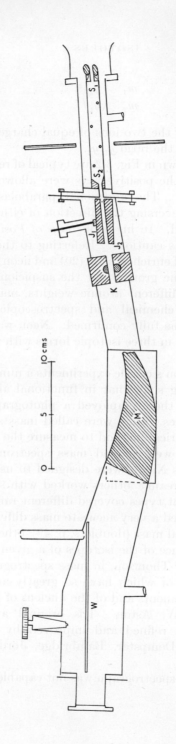

Fig. 3.3. Diagram of Aston's second mass spectrograph.

the deviations of the masses of isotopes from integral values. He therefore built the famous instrument, installed in the Cavendish laboratory in 1925, which measured mass values with an accuracy of one part in ten thousand. The details of this instrument may be seen in Fig. 3.3. A full account is to be found in Aston's book, *Mass Spectra and Isotopes* (1933). The *positive rays*, or *kanalstrahlen*, pass through a tube of narrow bore S_1 which pierces the cathode of a discharge tube, and then through a second collimating tube S_2. They then pass through an electric field, $J_1 J_2$, and are deflected through a small angle. After passing through a wide slit K they are deflected by a magnetic field M in the opposite direction and are received by a photographic plate W. There is a definite relation between the two angles of deflection ; when this holds, sharp images of all ions of the same mass are obtained on the photographic plate. With this instrument Aston discovered most of the existing stable isotopes and demonstrated that the masses of the nuclei, on the scale $^{16}O = 16$, differ from integral values by very small amounts.

Other investigators introduced refinements and obtained a higher order of accuracy. Reference may be made here to the spectrographs of Dempster and of Bainbridge. These are based on somewhat different principles which may be briefly described.

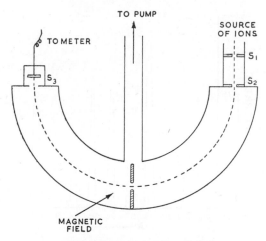

FIG. 3.4. Direction focusing.

E   H.N.S.

All mass spectrometers begin with a stream of ions issuing from a slit (S_2, Fig. 3.4). The ions differ from one another in the following respects : they have (1) different discrete masses, (2) different velocities, (3) different charges, which are multiples of the electron charge e and (4) different directions caused by the finite width of the slit S_2. The ions issuing from S_2 have been accelerated by a potential difference V (about 1000 volts) between S_1 and S_2. This produces an energy Ve in an ion having a charge e ; the energy may be equated to the resulting kinetic energy

$$Ve = \tfrac{1}{2}mv^2 \tag{3.6}$$

Thus, all singly ionised particles will have approximately the same energy irrespective of their mass.

The ions issuing from S_2 are caused to move in a circular path of radius ρ under the influence of a magnetic field B. The force acting on the ions, Bev, is always perpendicular to the path and is equal to the centrifugal force :

$$Bev = mv^2/\rho$$

that is, $$e/m = v/B\rho \tag{3.7}$$

Eliminating v from Eqs. (3.6) and (3.7),

$$e/m = 2V/B^2\rho^2 \tag{3.8}$$

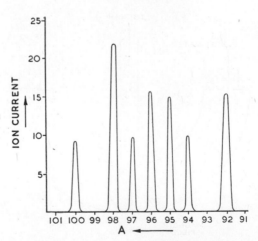

FIG. 3.5. Mass spectrum of molybdenum.

The slit S_3 (Fig. 3.4) is fixed in position so that if V and B are kept constant, only ions having a certain mass can enter the collector at S_3. As V is varied, $B\rho$ remaining constant, ions of a different mass per unit charge are caused to enter S_3 where an electrometer registers the strength of the ion current. The relative strength of the current is a measure of the relative abundance of the ions having a particular mass (Fig. 3.5).

Dempster's mass spectrometer makes use of this principle. One of its valuable features is that ions of the same value e/m, which issue from S_2 in slightly different directions, all enter the slit S_3. This may be seen by constructing circles of the same radius ρ but with centres above one another (Fig. 3.6). In Dempster's instrument, the ions were produced by bombardment by accelerated electrons of the atoms evaporated from the hot surface of the element under examination.

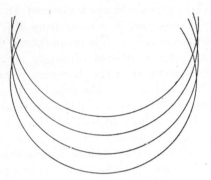

FIG. 3.6. Arcs of equal radii and collinear centres.

The method described above is known as *direction focusing*. The Bainbridge mass spectrograph, however, is a *velocity focusing* instrument. It makes use of a velocity filter (Fig. 3.7).

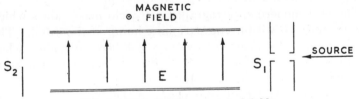

MAGNETIC FIELD

SOURCE

S_2 E S_1

FIG. 3.7. Velocity filter : crossed fields.

Ions of charge ne and of widely different velocities v leaving the slit S_1 may pass through the slit S_2, but in the presence of an electric field E they will be deflected by a force Ene. If a magnetic field B perpendicular to E is superimposed, the ions will be deflected by a force $Bnev$. By adjusting E and B so that the deflections are in opposite directions and $Ene = Bnev$, that is,

$$v = E/B, \qquad (3.9)$$

the ions may be caused to pass through S_2. Thus, all ions issuing from this slit, irrespective of their charge, have the same velocity. For this reason the device is called a " velocity selector " or " velocity filter ".

On issuing from S_2 the ions are deflected into a semi-circular path by a magnetic field of constant value ; their presence and relative position are registered by a photographic plate. Since v is constant, it is clear from Eq. (3.7) that the radius of the semi-circular path is proportional to m/e. Thus the determination of the masses of singly charged ions is reduced to the measurement of the distances between marks on a photograph plate. Moreover, the relative density of the lines on the plate provides a measure of the abundance of the isotopes.

In 1934 Mattauch of Austria combined direction focusing and velocity focusing in one mass spectrograph and obtained records capable of more accurate measurement than any hitherto produced. The twin advantages of widely spaced lines of high definition which is characteristic of direction focusing and the linear relation between the mass of the ion and the distance from a fiducial point of its record which is characteristic of velocity focusing were combined in the same instrument. The remarkable results obtained by Mattauch are illustrated in the Frontispiece* of this book which shows a fineness of line definition comparable with that of an optical spectrum.

The best modern spectrographs will yield mass values which are accurate to within one part in a hundred thousand. The great value of this degree of accuracy will become evident when we consider the binding energy of the nucleus and its bearing on nuclear stability and cognate topics (Chap. VII).

Space does not permit an account of the mass spectrometers which have been designed for special purposes, such as that of Nier (1947), which is adapted to the measurement of relative abundances and is comparatively cheap to construct, and that of Aston (1937), of Bainbridge and Jordan (1936), of Dempster

* From *Atomic Physics* (W. Finkelnburg)

(1935) and of Mattauch and Hertzog (1936). Mention must be made, however, of a method of measuring the records which has contributed to the accuracy of the results. It is called the *matched doublet* method.

Matched Doublets

The direct method of determining the mass of an isotope by measuring the distance of its trace on the photographic plate from that of ^{16}O has been superseded by the method of measuring the short distances between the records of ions having the same values of n/A, n being the multiplicity of ionisation. Two ions having the same n/A value will not have quite the same n/M values. They constitute what is called a *doublet*. The distance between the traces of their n/M values on the photographic plate is short and can be measured with great accuracy. The lines of a doublet should be matched in intensity for the best results. The mass of an isotope can then be made to depend on the matched doublet values in the way illustrated in the following example.

Table 3.1 records three mass doublets and their measured mass differences (Cohen and Hornyak, 1947). Note that here the subscripts to the symbols indicate the number of atoms in the molecule.

TABLE 3.1

Doublet	Symbol	A/n	Mass difference (mmu)
$^{1}H_2 - {}^{2}H$	α	2	$1 \cdot 539 \pm 0 \cdot 0021$
$^{2}H_3 - \frac{1}{2}{}^{12}C$	β	6	$42 \cdot 230 \pm 0 \cdot 019$
$^{12}C^{1}H_4 - {}^{16}O$	γ	16	$36 \cdot 369 \pm 0 \cdot 021$

From these three doublets, the mass differences of which, as the fourth column of Table 3.1 shows, are known with considerable accuracy (mmu = milli mass unit), the masses of the proton, the deuteron or of the nucleus of ^{12}C may be found immediately from the equations

$$^{1}H = \tfrac{1}{16}{}^{16}O + \tfrac{3}{8}\alpha + \tfrac{1}{8}\beta + \tfrac{1}{16}\gamma \qquad (3.10)$$

$$^{2}H = \tfrac{1}{8}{}^{16}O - \tfrac{1}{4}\alpha + \tfrac{1}{4}\beta + \tfrac{1}{8}\gamma \qquad (3.11)$$

$$^{12}C = \tfrac{3}{4}{}^{16}O - \tfrac{3}{2}\alpha - \tfrac{1}{2}\beta + \tfrac{3}{4}\gamma \qquad (3.12)$$

These equations may be verified by substituting for α, β, γ the chemical symbols from Table 3.1, remembering that the latter stand for masses. For example, Eq. 3.10 becomes

$$^1H = \tfrac{1}{16}{}^{16}O + \tfrac{3}{8}(^1H_2 - {}^2H) + \tfrac{1}{8}(^2H_3 - \tfrac{1}{2}{}^{12}C) + \tfrac{1}{16}(^{12}C^1H_4 - {}^{16}O)$$
$$= 1.000000 + 0.000577 + 0.005279 + 0.002273$$
$$= 1.008130 \text{ mu.} \tag{3.13}$$

The degree of accuracy obtainable by the matched doublet method is illustrated in Table 3.2 which gives the masses of four important nuclides (Cohen and Hornyak, 1947).

TABLE 3.2

Nuclide	Mass (mu)
^1H	1.0081284 ± 0.0000027
^2H	2.014718 ± 0.000005
^{12}C	12.003847 ± 0.000016
^{14}N	14.007539 ± 0.000015

The matched doublet method of determining nuclear masses may be expected to produce results of value in the future. If the accuracy of the measurements could be carried to one more decimal place it would be feasible to make direct measurements of the relatively small binding energy of the circumnuclear electrons.

The mass spectrograph affords the most direct means of measuring nuclear masses and it has hitherto proved fruitful. It is possible, however, to determine the masses of nuclei by methods which are *completely independent* of the mass spectrograph. The results are at present sufficiently exact to provide useful corroborative evidence but it is not impossible that in the future the alternative methods, with refinements resulting from experience, may excel that of the mass spectrograph in accuracy. One of these alternatives will be described in the following section.

II. *Nuclear Reactions*

The determination of the mass of an isotope by means of a nuclear reaction is dependent upon the measurement of the energy of the reaction. Chemists have long been familiar with the notion of *reaction energy*. The familiar chemical reaction

$$2H_2 + O_2 \rightarrow 2H_2O \tag{3.14}$$

proceeds with the evolution of heat and is therefore called an *exothermic* reaction. When heat is absorbed the reaction is said to be *endothermic*. The reaction may accordingly be expressed thus :

$$2H_2 + O_2 \rightarrow 2H_2O + Q \qquad (3.15)$$

where $Q = 136,000$ calories, and, for dimensional homogeneity, the symbols stand for the energy equivalents of molecular masses.

In 1932 Cockcroft and Walton brought about for the first time a nuclear reaction by means of particles which were artificially accelerated (Cockcroft and Walton, 1930 and 1932). For this they were awarded, in 1951, the Nobel prize for Physics. The reaction which they studied was

$$^7_3Li + ^1_1H + Q_1 (\rightarrow ^8_4Be) \rightarrow 2^4_2He + Q_2 \qquad (3.16)$$

It is to-day known also from cloud chamber, and from photographic emulsion experiments that when a proton having kinetic energy 0·4 MeV (Q_1) reacts with a ^7_3Li nucleus, an intermediate nucleus, is formed. This extremely unstable nucleus, ^8_4Be, splits into two α-particles recoiling in opposite directions with equal kinetic energies ($Q_2/2 = 8\cdot8$ MeV.) Eq. (3.16) may accordingly be written thus :

$$^7_3Li + ^1_1H \rightarrow 2^4_2He + Q \qquad (3.17)$$

where $\qquad Q = Q_2 - Q_1 = 17\cdot2$ MeV.

The analogy with the chemists' equation (3.15) is clear. Both reactions are exothermic, but the contrast in the amount of released energy is startling. It is the cause of the widespread interest in atomic energy. From Eq. (3.15) we know that when 4 gm. of hydrogen react chemically with 32 gm. of oxygen, 136,000 calories per mole are evolved. Eq. (3.17), on the other hand, shows that when 1 gm. of hydrogen interacts in a *nuclear* reaction with 7 gm. of lithium the evolution of energy is 397 *thousand million* calories per mole.

The important feature of Eq. (3.17) for the purpose of the present discussion is the balance of mass-energy, Q. According to the mass-energy equivalence relation $E = mc^2$ (Chap. VII), the sum of the masses of the nuclei (at rest) on the left-hand side of the equation must equal the sum of the masses of the two α-particles (at rest) on the right-hand side *plus the mass equiva-*

lent of the energy. From this it follows that, if this energy is known, the mass of any one of the three nuclei concerned in the reaction can be calculated from the masses of the other two.

Since 1932 the energies of a very large number of nuclear reactions have been measured. Another proton reaction, for example, which has been carefully studied is

$$^6_3Li + ^1_1H \rightarrow ^4_2He + ^3_2He + Q \qquad (3.18)$$

The Q-value of this reaction is found from measurements of the ranges of the two helium isotopes produced by a known kinetic energy of the incident proton. The mass-energy balance measurements are satisfactory.

Nuclear reactions initiated by a proton with the emission of a neutron—(p,n) reactions—provide a means of measuring nuclear masses with a considerable degree of accuracy because the difference in mass between a neutron and a proton is known to one part in 10^5 (Table 3.3).

TABLE (3.3)*

Particle	Atomic Mass (m u)	
	From Nuclear Data	From Mass Spectroscopy
n	$1 \cdot 008932(\pm 3)$	—
p	$1 \cdot 008142(\pm 3)$	$1 \cdot 008165(\pm 4)$
$n - p$	$0 \cdot 000790$	

Consider, for instance, the reaction

$$^{44}_{20}Ca + ^1_1H \rightarrow ^{44}_{21}Sc + n + Q \qquad (3.19)$$

If the mass of $^{44}_{20}Ca$ nucleus is known, that of the $^{44}_{21}Sc$ nucleus may be obtained from a careful measurement of Q, since the mass difference $^1_1H - n$ has been accurately determined.

The method of determining the masses of light nuclides from a knowledge of the disintegration energies of nuclear reactions promises to develop rapidly. The large number of Q-values of high accuracy now available allows the masses of light nuclei up to $A = 20$ to be determined without reference to the results obtained from mass spectroscopy. The possibility of this procedure was foreseen by H. A. Wilson in 1936. It has been

* Li et al., (1951).

developed by other investigators (Tollestrup *et al.*, 1950, Li *et al.*, 1951). The very large number of reactions, increasing every year, by which the light nuclides are interconnected provide an excess of cross-checks on the consistency of the Q-values, so that these values are over determined. These reactions are shown in Fig. 3.8. It is evident that the necessity

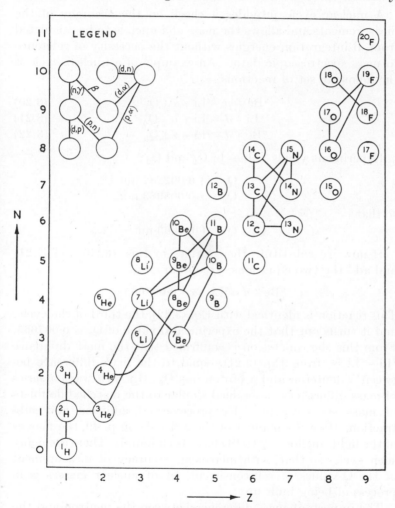

FIG. 3.8. Nuclear reactions equivalent to a combination of reactions.
(Lines connect target nucleus and residual nucleus.)

of self-consistency between the masses and Q-values of a set of nuclear reactions such as those shown in Fig. 3.8 is a source of accurate evaluation of nuclear masses. This will be clear from a consideration of what is termed a *nuclear cycle*.

Nuclear Cycles

A nuclear cycle provides a check on the accuracy of the measurements and allows the mass of a nuclide to be calculated from disintegration energies without the necessity of reference to mass spectroscopic data. An example of a nuclear cycle is the following set of reactions :

$$^9\text{Be} + p \rightarrow {}^6\text{Li} + \alpha + Q_1 \qquad (3.20)$$
$$^6\text{Li} + d \rightarrow {}^7\text{Li} + p + Q_2 \qquad (3.21)$$
$$^9\text{Be} + d \rightarrow {}^7\text{Li} + \alpha + Q_3 \qquad (3.22)$$

Experiment yields values of Q_1 and Q_2 :

$$Q_1 = +0.002282 \text{ mu}$$
$$Q_2 = +0.005383 \text{ mu}$$

so that

$$Q_1 + Q_2 = 0.007665 \text{ mu}$$

If now we substitute these values in Eqs. (3.20) and (3.21) and add the two equations, we obtain

$$^9\text{Be} + d \rightarrow {}^7\text{Li} + \alpha + 0.007665$$

This reaction is identical with Eq. (3.22), the third of the cycle, and it turns out that the experimental value of Q_3 is 0.007665. From this the conclusion is confirmed that the mass difference $^7\text{Li} - {}^6\text{Li}$ is, from Eq. (3.21), equal to the mass difference between a deuteron and a proton less Q_2. In such ways a series of mass differences is obtained similar to the matched doublets of mass spectroscopy. By processes of addition and subtraction, after the manner of the example on p. 49, the masses of the light nuclides up to ^{16}O have been found. There are many such cycles so that, with increasing accuracy of measurement of the Q-values, a self-consistent set of nuclear masses is in process of being built up.

The important mass difference between the neutron and the hydrogen atom may be determined by many different cycles.

The following is an example :

$$^3\text{H}\,(p,\,n)\;^3\text{He, energy}\;Q_1 \qquad (3.23)$$
$$^3\text{H}\,(\beta^-)\;^3\text{He, energy}\;Q_2 \qquad (3.24)$$
$$Q_1 = -\,0\cdot0008202\;\text{mu}$$
$$Q_2 = +\,0\cdot0000199\;\text{mu}$$

From (3.23) and (3.24) we obtain

$$n - {}^1\text{H} = 0\cdot0008401\;\text{mu} = 0\cdot782\;\text{MeV}.$$

A more complicated cycle which gives precisely the same result is, as expressed in the customary notation :

$$^{10}\text{B}\,(n,\,\alpha){}^7\text{Li},\;\;^9\text{Be}\,(d,\,\alpha){}^7\text{Li},\;\;^9\text{Be}\,(d,\,p){}^{10}\text{Be},\;\;^{10}\text{Be}\,(\beta^-){}^{10}\text{B}$$

The Q-values of these four reactions have been measured. From these data the value of $n - {}^1\text{H}$ is found, and that, be it noted, without reference to mass spectrograph measurements.

One method of directly determining the mass of the neutron is based on the observation that gamma rays of a certain minimum energy are able to split a deuterium nucleus into a proton and a neutron :

$$^2_1\text{H} + \gamma \rightarrow {}^1_1\text{H} + n \qquad (3.25)$$

This " threshold energy " is 2.21 MeV. which, from the mass-energy relation, is equivalent to $0\cdot00238$ mass units. Substituting masses for the symbols of Eq. (3.25),

$$2\cdot01472 + 0\cdot00238 = 1\cdot00813 + n,$$

whence the mass of the neutron is $1\cdot00897$ mu.

It is to be expected that the measurement of nuclear masses by measurements of the energy of nuclear reactions will become an increasingly fruitful field. More refined methods of estimating the energy and the increase in the number of cross checks provided by reaction cycles should result in a self-consistent set of isotope masses of an accuracy and reliability comparable with, if not superior to, those obtained by mass spectroscopy.

III. *Hyperfine Structure of Spectral Lines*

The lines of the optical spectrum of an element can be resolved by adequate spectroscopic resolving power into finer details : sets of lines called the *fine structure of the spectral lines*. This fine structure is a consequence of an interaction between the orbital electrons of the atom. In addition to this there is an interaction between the orbital electrons and the nucleus which depends upon the mass of the nucleus. In 1916 the ratio of the masses of the proton and electron was determined by measuring the small difference in the series constants of the Balmer series of the hydrogen spectrum and the Pickering series of the ionised helium spectrum, simple one-electron spectra. In an analogous manner the difference between the spectra of two isotopes of the same atomic number betrays a difference in the masses of the nuclei controlling the orbital electrons. This effect is very small, requiring for its detection the aid of interference spectroscopes of very high resolving power. It is known as *the hyperfine structure of spectral lines*. The effect was first discovered in the case of heavier atoms in 1931 (Schüler and Keyston, 1931) for the case of thallium. Many other examples have since been recognized. The existence of certain isotopes has indeed been established by this method before they were found by the mass spectrograph. Isotopes of iridium, platinum and lead were discovered in this way. The existence of the hydrogen isotope, deuterium, was demonstrated by Urey in 1932 by observation of the hyperfine structure produced by a mixture of the isotopes.

The causes of the hyperfine structure are multiple and complex. It is the isotope effect that concerns us here. It is known that, in the case of the hydrogen atom, Rydberg's constant and hence the wave-lengths of the hydrogen spectrum depend on the mass of the nucleus. If to this nucleus (the proton) is added a neutron, the result is the deuteron, the nucleus of the deuterium atom. Urey shewed in 1932 that the change in wavelength of the first line of the Balmer series was 1·79Å. In this way he confirmed the existence of an isotope of hydrogen. For heavy atoms this wavelength difference, due to the difference in mass of isotopes, becomes so small that it falls in the region of hyperfine structure.

As well as line spectra, band spectra have also revealed the presence of isotopes. If two molecules, such as ^{6}LiH and ^{7}LiH, contain atoms of different mass (^{6}Li and ^{7}Li), their moments of inertia will differ. The rotational and vibrational energy levels will affect their band spectra in differing degrees. Now the accuracy of optical spectroscopic measurement is very high so that a determination of the ratio of the intensity of the lines produced by the two types of molecule yields information concerning the relative abundance of the isotopes. In this way new isotopes of carbon, nitrogen and oxygen were discovered and the existence of many isotopes which the mass spectroscope had detected was confirmed and their masses and relative abundances have been measured.

Very recently an entirely new method of studying molecules which promises to have a useful bearing on the study of isotopes has been found. This is *microwave spectroscopy*. The development between 1940 and 1945 of microwave techniques in the region of the spectrum covered by the range of wave-lengths 1 mm. to 20 cm. is now a subject of intensive study (Gordy, 1948). Only absorption methods are used. The very high frequency waves are passed through a vapour of the molecules under investigation and the absorption of energy at different frequencies is measured. From this precise values of nuclear separations, the moments of inertia of molecules, quadrupole coupling coefficients, nuclear spins and other information is obtainable. Some of these results—for example, the molecular moments of inertia—depend on the nuclear masses so that the study provides evidence of the existence, and of the relative abundance of isotopes. The method is not as direct as that of mass spectroscopy but it is very sensitive and is capable of producing results of a high order of accuracy. It may be anticipated that it will be increasingly valuable in the study of nuclear mass.

Separation of Isotopes

The separation of the isotopes of an element is an important and difficult practical problem. The difficulties will become clearer as we consider what is involved. The importance of the problem lies in the circumstance that an element enriched in one of its isotopes has useful experimental and technical applications such as, for example, the use of stable isotopes as tracers. The enrichment of uranium in its $^{235}_{92}U$ isotope is fundamental to current atomic energy projects. The concentration of deuterium has made possible many fruitful laboratory experiments.

Several methods of enriching an element with one of its isotopes have been applied successfully. These are : (a) the electromagnetic method, (b) the gaseous diffusion method, (c) the thermal diffusion method, (d) the centrifugal method, (e) the distillation method, (f) the chemical exchange method and (g) the electrolytic method. The first of these is the only one that effects 100 per cent separation. It is in its essentials the method of the mass spectrograph. But the quantity separated is measured in milligrams. The other methods achieve only a partial separation of isotopes.

Gaseous Diffusion Method

The first method by which an enrichment of isotopes was effected was by gaseous diffusion : Graham discovered in 1840 that the rate of diffusion of a gas is inversely proportional to the square root of its density. Thus the lighter of two isotopes of a gas will diffuse more rapidly through a porous membrane than the heavier. Aston announced at the British Association Meeting in 1913 the partial separation of the neon isotopes by diffusion through the walls of a pipe-clay tube. From Graham's law it is evident that the efficiency of the diffusion process is greatest in the case of the hydrogen isotopes where the separation rate is as $\sqrt{2/1}$ or 1·4. For neon it is $\sqrt{22/20}$ or 1·049. The efficiency decreases rapidly with increasing atomic mass, but it can be augmented by the " cascade " method in which the enriched gaseous isotope is subjected to successive stages of diffusion. Hertz used the cascade method in developing an apparatus applied, in 1932, to the separation of the neon isotopes. Forty-eight tubes and many refinements achieved a separation of 99 per cent of 55 c.c. of $^{20}_{10}$Ne in eight hours—a considerable achievement.

The cascade method was the method employed to concentrate the 235 isotope of uranium, in the gaseous form of uranium hexafluoride, for use in the atomic bomb. This enterprise was the largest undertaking of chemical engineering ever planned. An account of it is to be found in the Smyth *Report* (1945).

Other Methods

The electromagnetic method, by which is achieved 100 per cent isolation of small quantities of isotopes, is in essence that of the Dempster mass spectrograph (Fig. 3.9). The vapour of the

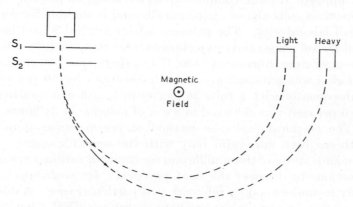

FIG. 3.9. Electromagnetic separation of isotopes.

compound formed from the isotopes is bombarded by an electron stream. The ions, after passing through the slits S_1 and S_2 between which is an accelerating field V_1 are compelled by a magnetic field H_0, which is perpendicular to the plane of the figure, to traverse semi-circular paths of radius r determined by the mass of the ion according to the equation

$$\frac{H_0^2 r^2}{2v} = \frac{m}{e}. \tag{3.26}$$

Collectors are placed in appropriate positions to collect the separated isotopes. Since m is proportional to H_0^2, Eq. (3.26) shows that a variation by a factor 6 in the value of H_0 covers a range of isotope masses from $A = 6$ to $A = 216$.

The experimental observation in which the thermal diffusion method originated is that in a vessel where a steep temperature gradient exists the gas at the higher temperature contains a slightly higher concentration of the lighter molecules. The essential feature of a thermal diffusion plant is a vertical cylinder, containing the element in gaseous form, down the centre of which runs a hot wire or tube. The wire may be kept at a temperature of 500° C. while the walls of the tube are cold. Partial separation of the isotopes is then effected by thermal convection. The heavier isotope tends to collect at the bottom of the tube and the lighter at the top. The cascade process may be applied, several columns in series being employed. The apparatus runs almost automatically and is suitable for use in small laboratories. The pioneers in this method were Clusius and Dickel whose early experiments were made in 1938. With a temperature difference of 600° C. in a single tube 300 cm. long, chlorine was enriched in one of its isotopes by 50 per cent. Subsequently with a tube 36 metres in length a separation of 99·6 per cent was achieved in 8 c.c. of chlorine in 24 hours.

The chemical exchange method of isotope separation has hitherto been successful only with the lighter elements. It demands study of the equilibrium constants of various exchange reactions to discover the most practical. Its *modus operandi* may be understood by reference to a particular case. A downward flow of ammonium sulphate containing $^{14}NH_3^+$ ions in a vertical tube is met by an upward stream of bubbles of ammonia gas. There is an interchange of heavy and light isotopes in accordance with the reaction

$$^{14}NH_3 \quad + \quad ^{15}NH_4^+ \quad \rightleftharpoons \quad ^{15}NH_3 \quad + \quad ^{14}NH_4^+$$
(light ammonia gas) (heavy sulphate ion) (heavy ammonia gas) (light sulphate ion)

Experiment shows that when the equilibrium represented by this equation is reached, the ratio of concentration of the light nitrogen isotope in the gas to the heavy is 1·02. This factor is sufficient to make a cascade process feasible and an enrichment of ^{15}N of more than 50 per cent has been achieved in this way.

It is improbable that any of the methods now in use can be developed to effect a 100 per cent isolation of an isotope *in quantity*, except in the well-known cases in which the enterprise is backed by the financial resources of a nation. Nevertheless, the partial separation which can be achieved by the methods described has had useful applications. An element enriched in one of its isotopes has many and various uses in tracer experiments as well as in investigations of those characteristic physical and spectroscopic properties of the isotope which throw light on its nuclear constitution.

REFERENCES

F. W. Aston, 1937, *P.R.S.*, A. 163, 391.
K. T. Bainbridge and E. B. Jordan, 1936, *Phys. Rev.*, 50, 282.
B. B. Boltwood, 1906, *Am. J. Sci.*, 22, 537.
J. D. Cockcroft and E. T. S. Walton, 1930, *P.R.S.*, A. 129, 477.
J. D. Cockcroft and E. T. S. Walton, 1932, *P.R.S.*, A. 136, 619.
Cohen and Hornyak, 1947, *Phys. Rev.*, 72, 1127.
A. J. Dempster, 1935, *Proc. Am. Phil. Soc.*, 75, 755.
Gordy, 1948, *Rev. Mod. Phys.*, 20, 668.
C. W. Li *et al.*, 1951, *Phys. Rev.*, 83, 512.
J. Mattauch and Hertzog, 1936, *Phys. Rev.*, 50, 617.
A. O. Nier (1947), *Rev. Sci. Instr.*, 18, 398.
Schüler and Keyston, 1931, *Z. f. Physik.*, 70, 1.
H. D. Smyth, 1945, *Atomic Energy for Military Purposes.*
S. G. Starling, 1946, *Electricity and Magnetism*, p. 498.
A. V. Tollestrup *et al.*, 1950, *Phys. Rev.*, 78, 372.

CHAPTER IV

THE NATURAL NUCLIDES :
EMPIRICAL RULES

An interesting and useful way of representing visually the whole family of nuclides, having regard to their nucleonic structure, is by means of a chart in which each nuclide is represented by a single point the abscissa of which is Z, the number of protons, and the ordinate of which is $N (= A - Z)$, the number of neutrons in the nuclide. Such a diagram for the natural nuclides is shown in Fig. 4.1. This method of representation is made more informative by expanding each point into a rectangle, rhombus or hexagon (Sullivan, 1949) and exhibiting in each area details of the mass, relative abundance, stability and other properties of the nuclide proper to that area. Such a diagram, as well as that typified in Fig. 4.1, is known as an Isotopic Chart or a Chart of the Nuclides. In these pages it will often be referred to as a ZN diagram.

The ZN Diagram

In such a chart the spaces representing the *isotopes* of any element lie on a line ($Z = $ constant) which is parallel to the N-axis ; the *isotones* corresponding to a given value of N are found on lines ($N = $ constant) which are parallel to the Z-axis ; and the loci of *isobars*, corresponding to a given value of A, are lines of negative slope which are equally inclined to the Z- and the N-axes. In Fig. 5.1 the isobaric lines are indicated by the mass numbers attached to them.

We shall have occasion in later pages to select restricted sections of the chart of the isotopes in order to consider them in detail but for the present the aim is to look at the members of the family of nuclides *as a whole* and to draw attention to certain interesting and significant features of the chart. It will be found that this particular method of representing the isotopes brings into clearer view a number of rules and regularities of which some are evident from a glance at the chart while others are not visually represented. These empirical rules, being based on the ZN diagram, are of course related to the hypothesis that the nuclide is composed of two sorts of particles, the charged and uncharged nucleons of the nucleus. They must consequently be integrated into any valid nuclear theory.

The chart of the stable nuclides includes 276 species and is probably complete. Based as it is on the results of a very large number of experiments by nuclear physicists carried on during the first half of the twentieth century, it is one of the significant tabulations of modern physics, to be ranked in importance with the chemists' periodic classification of the elements. It should be habitual for the physicist to take a general mental view of the ZN diagram and to consider a nuclide in relation to it even as the chemist always has the periodic table in mind as he relates an element to it. The periodic table reveals recurrent regularities which are significant of the chemical properties of the elements. The chart of the nuclides exhibits regularities which are interpreted in terms of the structure and properties of the nuclei. As the theory of atomic structure is designed to explain the features of the periodic classification of the elements, so any theory of the constitution of the nucleus and of the forces operating between nuclear particles must be adequate to interpret the regularities which are made evident by the nuclidic chart.

Empirical Rules

The visual representation of the elements according to the periodic classification has taken many forms, culminating in the modern three-dimensional spiral which is rich in significance. The isotopic chart has also been progressively improved. In its most recent representation it reveals a variety of nuclear features such as the composition of nuclei, their stability, their relative abundance when stable, the type of their activity when unstable, their mass and mass number, their spin and their relation to other nuclei. All these properties may be visually exhibited. These systematics of the nuclides are summarised in the following pages in a number of empirical rules.

Of the various methods of representing the family of isotopes that of Fig. 4.1 is probably the most generally useful. Based on the accepted hypothesis of nuclear structure, it shows at a glance the nucleonic composition of any isotope in terms of protons and neutrons. The isobaric diagonals (see Fig. 5.1) show the masses of the isotopes and the general trend of the variation of A with Z. The increase of isotopic number $(N - Z)$ with increasing Z is clearly in evidence. The change with Z of the " spread " of the isotopes is also shown. The " spread " is a maximum in the neighbourhood of $Z = 50$. The chart shows that, with two exceptions, all nuclides from $Z = 0$ to $Z = 92$ occur naturally. The exceptions are nuclides of atomic numbers 43 and 61. Reasons for anticipating that these two gaps correspond to unstable nuclides will be given later (p. 135).

There are other useful methods of charting the family of nuclides. It is sometimes convenient to plot mass number A as abscissa *versus* atomic number Z as ordinate. The isobars are then found on lines parallel to the ordinates while the isotopes occur on the diagonals. Another method of plotting takes mass number A as abscissa and isotopic number $(N - Z)$ as ordinate. This produces a long narrow chart convenient to fold. We reaffirm, however, that, while each of these methods has its advantages, the ZN chart has probably the most general application being based most obviously on the proton-neutron hypothesis of nuclear structure.

While it is true, as has been mentioned, that the chart of the natural isotopes is probably complete in the sense that the discovery of additional naturally occurring isotopes is improbable, it should be borne in mind that the chart itself is not static : it varies slowly with time. Had the terrestrial nuclides been charted a few million years ago, the representation must have included members of the neptunium radioactive family, long since decayed. In the same way some of the isotopes now shown in Fig. 4.1 are radioactive. By their slow decay they will in the course of ages cease to exist on the earth. It is not only the heaviest elements $(Z > 82)$ which are in process of decay ; a few elements of smaller atomic number such as samarium $(^{152}_{62}Sm)$, potassium $(^{40}_{19}K)$ and others are slowly disappearing. Indeed, the possibility must be reckoned with that many naturally occurring elements regarded as stable are in fact feebly radioactive, though the activity is too small to be registered by methods hitherto developed.

That the chart of the isotopes is not static and final but is subject to continuous, slow change through the centuries may appear to be a matter of little importance, but it is very relevant to a topic of great interest to cosmologists. The relative quantities of a radioactive nuclide and its products which occur in nature are data which bear directly on the question of the age of the galaxy in which the solar system has its place as well as on the cognate topic of the age of the elements (Chap. XII).

Let us now take a broad view of the whole group of nuclides from $Z=0$ to $Z=92$. Each of these, with two exceptions, is a family of from one to ten natural isotopes. In such a general survey a number of interesting regularities are to be observed. Some of these are evident from a glance at Fig. 4.1 ; others cannot be visually represented.

It is unlikely that a satisfactory theory of the nucleus will be *simple*. It would be contrary to all experience of the micro-cosmos that any account of the nucleus which corresponded closely to the facts could be pictorially represented as may be done with the data of the macrocosmos. At the same time some rough and ready model must be suggested, not only to satisfy a mental craving but also to assist in marshalling the experimental facts into order. Whether it be the nuclear shell or the liquid drop or some other concept of the sub-atomic structure, it may serve as an approximation to a reality which, because of the limitations of the powers of human imagining, cannot adequately be pictured. With this admittedly imperfect model it should be possible to account in a qualitative manner for some of the regularities of the isotopic chart. These regularities or systematics of the nuclides will be stated as "*Rules*" and in this and the succeeding chapter will be examined in turn.

Rule 1. *The natural nuclides are divisible into three groups in which mass is roughly correlated with stability : (i) light nuclides having stability related to atomic number ; (ii) medium weight nuclides of maximum and uniform stability ; (iii) heavy, unstable nuclides.*

The grouping is evident in the graph of the binding energy of a nucleus *versus* its mass number (p. 117). The dividing line between the second and third groups is clearly marked, the last nuclide of group (ii) being mercury ($Z = 80$). The section between groups (i) and (ii) is not quite so definite but it may be taken to occur in the vicinity of calcium ($Z = 20$).

The relation of binding energy to mass number is discussed in Chap. VII, but some important points may be noted here. For small mass numbers—group (i)—there is a periodic variation in nuclear binding energy as the mass number increases. Nuclides which contain equal numbers of protons and neutrons are exceptionally stable, e.g., $_2^4$He, $_6^{12}$C, $_8^{16}$O. It is difficult to remove a nucleon from one of these nuclides. They mark the position of minima in the plot of (negative) binding energy as ordinate against mass number as abscissa (Fig. 7.3). This fact may be interpreted on the hypothesis that two protons and two neutrons (an alpha particle sub-group) form a " shell " at a low level of energy. The large binding energy of the alpha particle (28.2 MeV.) is a measure of its great stability.

For nuclides of medium mass—group (ii)—the binding energy is a maximum and nearly constant at 8·5 MeV. per nucleon. These nuclides consequently have the greatest stability, the maximum occurring in the neighbourhood of the transition elements, iron ($Z = 26$), cobalt ($Z = 27$) and nickel ($Z = 28$). As the atomic number increases, the electrostatic (Coulomb) forces of repulsion between the protons become increasingly influential and the binding energy diminishes slowly until in the neighbourhood of mercury ($Z = 80$) instability sets in.

The Coulomb energy is unsaturated. Existing between pairs of protons it is roughly proportional to $\frac{1}{2}Z(Z-1)/r$ where r is the radius of the nucleus. Since r varies as $A^{\frac{1}{3}}$ (Chap. II), the disruptive Coulomb energy is proportional (approximately) to $Z^2/A^{\frac{1}{3}}$. Comparing the energy for $_{80}^{200}$Hg with that for $_{20}^{40}$Ca we obtain a ratio of about 10 : 1.

The variation of Coulomb energy per nucleon with increasing atomic number is shown in Fig. 4.2. It is evident that for the heavy nuclides the neutralization of the binding energy of

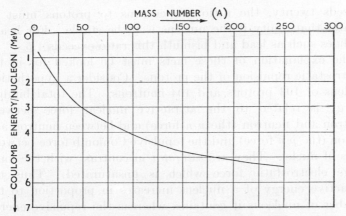

FIG. 4.2. Average Coulomb energy per nucleon v. mass number.

nucleons by the electrostatic energy is a factor of decisive importance.

Rule 2. In any light nuclide (up to $Z = 20$), the number of neutrons (N) is approximately equal to the number of protons (Z). Beyond $Z = 20$ the excess of neutrons over protons increases with increasing atomic number.

The line $N = Z$ shown in Fig. 4.1 is followed by the light stable nuclides as far as $Z = 20$. Beyond this the " line of stability " lies above the line $N = Z$. This fact may be expressed by saying that the isotopic number of a nuclide $I (= N - Z)$ is zero for several nuclides up to and including $Z = 20$, after which it is positive and increases with Z. Apart from the hydrogen nucleus only one stable nuclide has a negative isotopic number, viz., $_2^3\text{He}$ for which $I = -1$. The great majority of stable nuclides have a positive isotopic number. The statistics are given in Table 4.1.

TABLE 4.1

Z	$I = N - Z$	No. of Nuclides
1 and 2	-1	2
2 to 20	0	11
21 to 92	>0	263

It appears that, when the number of protons in a nucleus

exceeds twenty, the ratio of neutrons to protons must be greater than unity if the nucleus is to be stable. For heavy nuclides such as lead and bismuth this ratio exceeds 1.5.

The explanation of these facts must be looked for in the electrostatic repulsion of the protons. Consider a hypothetical nucleus of 104 protons and 104 neutrons. The total binding energy is related to the attractive nuclear force between neutron and neutron (the n-n force) and between neutron and proton (the p-n force) and the repulsive Coulomb force between pairs of nuclei. They are *saturated* in contrast with the long-range electrostatic force which is unsaturated. Thus the attractive energy of a nucleus increases in proportion to the number of nucleons it contains, whereas the repulsive energy increases as the square of the number of protons. The hypothetical nucleus $^{208}_{104}X$ is unstable. By changing a proton into a neutron ($^{208}_{103}Y$) the n-n and p-n forces are increased and the Coulomb force is diminished. It is not, however, until 22 protons of this hypothetical nuclide are transformed into neutrons that stability is reached : $^{208}_{82}Pb$ is the most abundant isotope of lead. In this nuclide the electrostatic forces of repulsion are reduced to a level below that of the nuclear forces, the neutron to proton ratio being 1·54.

It is not understood why the limit of naturally occurring nuclides is found at $Z = 92$ but it is in some way a consequence of the natural instability of heavier nuclei which are susceptible of alpha decay, which is relatively rapid, or of fission.

Rule 3. *Nuclei with both Z and N ($= A - Z$) even are by far the most numerous species. The number of nuclei with Z even and N odd is about equal to the number with Z odd and N even. Nuclei with both Z and N odd are rare.*

The quantitative expression of this Rule is in Table 4.2.

TABLE 4.2

Neutrons (N)		Protons (Z)	
		Even	Odd
	Even	162	52
	Odd	56	4

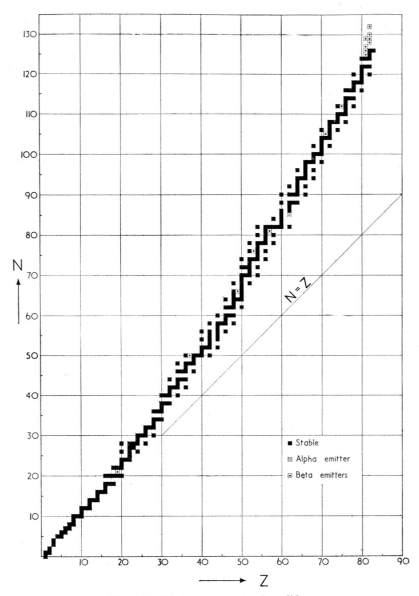

Fig. 4.1. *ZN* diagram : natural nuclides.

The Table shows that nuclei of even Z are more numerous than nuclei of odd Z in the ratio 218 : 56 or approximately 4 : 1. Nuclei of even mass number, $A (=Z+N)$ are more numerous than those of odd A in the ratio 166 : 108. All nuclei with even A, except four, have even Z. The four exceptions are all light nuclei : ^2_1H, ^6_3Li, $^{10}_5B$, $^{14}_7N$. ($^{40}_{19}K$ and $^{176}_{71}Lu$ are not stable but feebly β-radioactive. The same applies to $^{50}_{23}V$ and probably to $^{138}_{57}La$). If A is odd, nuclei with even Z and odd Z are about equally numerous in the ratio 14 : 13.

The foregoing comparisons must not be misunderstood. They are based merely on a count of the stable isotopes shown in the ZN diagram (Fig. 4.1) and have no reference to the relative abundance of the isotopes in nature. Nevertheless, it would be natural to expect from the numerical excess of nuclei with even Z and even N that these would be the most stable and therefore most abundant. The expectation is justified : the elements corresponding to $^{16}_8O$, $^{24}_{12}Mg$, $^{28}_{14}Si$, $^{40}_{20}Ca$, $^{48}_{22}Ti$ and $^{56}_{26}Fe$ form about 80 per cent of the earth's crust.

A qualitative explanation of these Rules is based on an application of the Pauli exclusion principle to nucleons. We suppose that two protons or two neutrons may occupy the same nuclear energy level provided that they have antiparallel spins. Thus we may expect, in analogy with the case of electron shells, that a closed nuclear state consists of two protons and two neutrons, each pair having oppositely directed spins. If, further, each nucleon interacts strongly with others in the same state and weakly with others in a different state, the saturation characteristic of nuclear forces is accounted for.

In analogy with electron shells, it is to be anticipated that nuclei with closed shells will have superior stability. The simplest example is the α-particle with two protons and two neutrons. Other examples are $^{12}_6C$ and $^{16}_8O$ both of which have unusually large binding energies. It is noteworthy that the nuclides mentioned above as constituting 80 per cent of the lithosphere have mass numbers which are multiples of four.

By the time the number of nucleons exceeds 40, the Coulomb repulsion effect is strongly in evidence. The addition of a pair of neutrons with opposite spins will tend to greater stability than will the addition of a pair of protons. A single proton or neutron will be less strongly bound. Hence, nuclei with even Z and even N are likely to be stable, in agreement with the observed greater frequency of their occurrence.

There are only four stable nuclei of the odd-odd type : $^2_1$H, $^6_3$Li, $^{10}_5$B, $^{14}_7$N. Nuclei of mass number greater than 14 having both Z and N odd are unstable. A qualitative explanation of this observation is based on the electrostatic repulsion of protons, which is an unsaturated force. The four odd-odd nuclides have a composition which may be represented by the formula $(pnpn)_\omega pn$ where $\omega = 0, 1, 2$ or 3. The odd pn will not react with the closed $(pnpn)$ but the p-n nuclear interaction may be supposed to be sufficient to counteract the Coulomb forces between the protons until $\omega > 3$. The nucleus $(pnpn)_4 pn$ is unstable : $^{18}_9$F is a positron emitter with a half-life of 1·92 hours. The addition of one *neutron*, however, to $(pnpn)_4 pn$ is sufficient to counteract the electrostatic forces : $^{19}_9$F is stable. Similarly, $(pnpn)_5 pn$ is unstable : $^{22}_{11}$Na is a positron emitter with a half-life of 3 years. Adding a neutron produces $^{23}_{11}$Na, the only stable isotope of sodium. Continuing in this way we find that the addition of a single neutron to the nucleus $(pnpn)_\omega pn$ is sufficient for stability until $\omega = 10$, the nucleus now containing 21 protons. Hereafter, for $\omega > 10$, *three* additional neutrons are required to counteract the Coulomb forces : $^{45}_{21}$Sc is stable. To maintain stability, as Z increases N must increase more rapidly. Thus, odd-odd nuclei with $A > 14$ are radioactive, emitting either negatrons or positrons until the appropriate N/Z ratio for stability is attained.

Rule 4 (*a*). *Elements with even Z frequently have several stable isotopes with even A but very few with odd A.*

Rule 4 (*b*). *Elements with odd Z never have more than two isotopes and these (except $^2_1$H, $^6_3$Li, $^{10}_5$B and $^{14}_7$N) have odd mass number. No element except tin ($Z = 50$) has more than two isotopes of odd mass number ; these numbers always differ by two.*

This well-known Rule was discovered by Aston. It may be verified immediately by an examination of the ZN diagram. If Z and A are even, the numbers of protons and neutrons are both even. The diagram shows, for example, that there are *seven* stable isotopes with A even for $Z=50$, *six* for $Z=52$ and *seven* for $Z=54$. On the other hand, if Z is even and A is *odd*, there is an odd neutron. Then, with the exceptions shown in Table 4.3, there is, for $Z=2$, 4, 6...40, only one stable isotope with A odd for each value of Z. For $Z=42$, 44, 46...82, there are two stable isotopes with A odd for each value of Z.

TABLE 4.3

(Exceptions referred to in text)

Z	Number of Isotopes
18	0
22	2
46	1
50	3
58	0
68	1
74	1
78	1
82	1

Thus, the 41 stable elements having Z even and A odd—containing, therefore, one odd neutron—have only 58 isotopes between them. Tin $(Z=50)$ is the only stable isotope with even Z and odd A which has as many as three isotopes. When the mass number is odd, elements with even Z are about as numerous as elements with odd Z.

Rule 5. The range of mass number, or the spread, of isotopes of even mass number is much greater than that of isotopes of odd mass number.

This Rule may be illustrated by reference to the nine isotopes of xenon $(Z=54)$:

Even mass numbers   124 126 128   130   132 134 136
Odd mass numbers   129   131

It is evident that in a stable element having an odd number of neutrons the range of neutron to proton ratio deduced from its nucleonic composition is very small. If the ratio falls above or below certain narrow limits, negatron instability, by which a neutron is changed into a proton, or positron instability by which a proton becomes a neutron, occurs. For elements with even mass number, also, there is for stability an optimum, essentially single-valued, ratio of N to Z. In the case of xenon this ratio lies between 1·29 and 1·52. For increasing Z there is a gradual increase in the value of N/Z. This relation is represented by a line on the ZN diagram known as the line of stability. It is discussed in Chap. V.

Table 4.4, which is extracted from the middle of the ZN diagram, serves to illustrate Rules 4 and 5.

TABLE 4.4

Z		Number of Isotopes		
		A		Total
odd	even	odd	even	
47		2	0	2
	48	2	6	8
49		2	0	2
	50	3	7	10
51		2	0	2
	52	2	5	7
53		1	0	1
	54	2	7	9

Further empirical rules summarising regularities among the isotopes will be discussed in the next chapter after a reference to the artificial isotopes. The latter are more numerous than the natural isotopes and require separate consideration. Each artificial isotope finds its place in the extended ZN diagram, on one side or the other of the line of stability. The aim will continue to be a general survey of the whole family of nuclides which will now include the more numerous artificial nuclides. What may be called the Systematics of the Nuclides, as summarised in the Isotope Rules of these two chapters, is a topic of great interest in itself apart altogether from its theoretical explanation. At present no satisfactory explanation covering all the empirical Rules exists, but this is not a novel situation in the history of Science. The empirical rules of planetary motion given by Kepler before Newton showed them to be a consequence of gravitational attraction, and the empirical relation between the frequencies of the lines of the hydrogen spectrum announced by Balmer before they were interpreted by the Bohr theory of the atom, are examples of rules which possessed an interest of their own apart from the theory which subsequently explained them.

REFERENCE

W. H. Sullivan, 1949, *Trilinear Chart of Nuclear Species.*

CHAPTER V

STABLE AND UNSTABLE NUCLIDES :
MORE EMPIRICAL RULES

THE customary classification of the nuclides into two categories, *natural* and *artificial*, demands a word of explanation. By *natural nuclide* is meant a nuclide which, whether stable or unstable, is found in the crust of the earth. An *artificial nuclide* is a species which is produced by mechanical means, usually by the disintegration of stable atoms which undergo bombardment by other stable particles. These are also " natural " in that they are to be found in the stars, but the definitions have reference to nuclides which either occur naturally or are produced artificially on this planet. It follows that natural nuclides include many radioactive isotopes belonging to the uranium, actinium and thorium series. The neptunium series of radioactive isotopes, although occurring naturally in the early stages of the earth's history, has long since decayed and, since it is now produced in the laboratory or the atomic pile, must be classed as artificial.

TABLE 5.1

ISOTOPES OF THE STABLE ELEMENTS : MASS NUMBERS

Element	Atomic No. (Z)	Isotopes (A)	Element	Atomic No. (Z)	Isotopes (A)
Hydrogen -	1	1, 2	Aluminium -	13	27
Helium -	2	3, 4	Silicon -	14	28, 29, 30
Lithium -	3	6, 7	Phosphorus -	15	31
Beryllium -	4	9	Sulphur -	16	32, 33, 34, 36
Boron -	5	10, 11	Chlorine -	17	36, 37
Carbon -	6	12, 13	Argon -	18	36, 38, 40
Nitrogen -	7	14, 15	Potassium -	19	39, 40,* 41
Oxygen -	8	16, 17, 18	Calcium -	20	40, 42, 43, 46, 48
Fluorine -	9	19	Scandium -	21	45
Neon -	10	20, 21, 22	Titanium -	22	46, 47, 48, 49, 50
Sodium -	11	23	Vanadium -	23	50,† 51
Magnesium -	12	24, 25, 26	Chromium -	24	50, 52, 53, 54

* Radioactive.   † Probably radioactive.

TABLE 5.1—continued

Element	Atomic No. (Z)	Isotopes (A)	Element	Atomic No. (Z)	Isotopes (A)
Manganese	- 25	55	Lanthanum	- 57	138,† 139
Iron	- 26	54, 56, 57, 58	Cerium	- 58	136, 138, 140,
Cobalt	- 27	59			142
Nickel	- 28	58, 60, 61, 62, 64	Praseodymium	59	141
Copper	- 29	63, 65	Neodymium	- 60	142, 143, 144,
Zinc	- 30	64, 66, 67, 68, 70			145, 146, 148,
Gallium	- 31	69, 71			150 *
Germanium	- 32	70, 72, 73, 74, 76	Promethium	- 61	—
Arsenic	- 33	75	Samarium	- 62	144, 147, 148,
Selenium	- 34	74, 76, 77, 78,			149, 150, 152,*
		80, 82			154
Bromine	- 35	79, 81	Europium	- 63	151, 153
Krypton	- 36	78, 80, 82, 83,	Gadolinium	- 64	152, 154, 155,
		84, 86			156, 157, 158,
Rubidium	- 37	85, 87*			160
Strontium	- 38	84, 86, 87, 88	Terbium	- 65	159
Yttrium	- 39	89	Dysprosium	- 66	156, 158, 160,
Zirconium	- 40	90, 91, 92, 94, 96			161, 162, 163,
Columbium	- 41	93			164
Molybdenum	- 42	92, 94, 95, 96,	Holmium	- 67	165
		97, 98, 100	Erbium	- 68	162, 164, 166,
Technetium	- 43	—			167, 168, 170
Ruthenium	- 44	96, 98, 99, 100,	Thulium	- 69	169
		101, 102, 104	Ytterbium	- 70	168, 170, 171,
Rhodium	- 45	103			172, 173, 174,
Palladium	- 46	102, 104, 105,			176
		106, 108, 110	Lutetium	- 71	175, 176 *
Silver	- 47	107, 109	Hafnium	- 72	174, 176, 177,
Cadmium	- 48	106, 108, 110,			178, 179, 180
		111, 112, 113,	Tantalum	- 73	181
		114, 116	Tungsten	- 74	180, 182, 183,
Indium	- 49	113, 115 *			184, 186
Tin	- 50	112, 114, 115,	Rhenium	- 75	185, 187 *
		116, 117, 118,	Osmium	- 76	184, 186, 187,
		119, 120, 122,			188, 189, 190,
		124			192
Antimony	- 51	121, 123	Iridium	- 77	191, 193
Tellurium	- 52	120, 122, 123,	Platinum	- 78	190, 192, 194,
		124, 125, 126,			195, 196, 198
		128, 130	Gold	- 79	197
Iodine	- 53	127	Mercury	- 80	196, 198, 199,
Xenon	- 54	124, 126, 128,			200, 201, 202,
		129, 130, 131,			204
		132, 134, 136	Thallium	- 81	203, 205
Cæsium	- 55	133	Lead	- 82	204, 206, 207,
Barium	- 56	130, 132, 134,			208
		135, 136, 137,	Bismuth	- 83	209
		138			

* Radioactive,   † Probably radioactive.

Table 5.1 lists the natural isotopes excluding the radioactive elements from $Z = 84$ to $Z = 92$. Although styled " Isotopes of the Stable Elements ", it includes the following unstable isotopes of very long half-lives, each marked with an asterisk.

Alpha-active :   Samarium (152)
Beta-active :   Potassium (40), Rubidium (87)
                            Indium (115), Neodymium (150)
                            Lutetium (176), Rhenium (187)
Possibly beta-active : Vanadium (50), Lanthanum (138).

The table lists 280 nuclides. With the 40 alpha emitters the natural nuclides number about 320 species. The number of nuclides produced by artificial means increases year by year. So far the total is about 700 so that altogether more than 1000 isotopes of the 92 elements are known. The Table shows that 21 of the elements, about one quarter of the whole number, consist of single isotopes, all the others being mixtures of at least two isotopes, one or two, such as tin, having as many as ten isotopes in their composition.

The Line of Stability

Fig. 5.1 is a plot of the known nuclides, natural and artificial. It may be compared with Fig. 4.1 which shows the stable nuclides. What is called the *line of stability* is clearly indicated. There is a striking tendency for all the stable nuclides to lie contiguously within a narrow band, the width of which is a measure of the limits of stability.

For light nuclides the slope of the line of stability is 45°, the N/Z ratio being unity. For heavier nuclides, since N/Z increases with Z up to a value of about 1·5, the line of stability diverges more and more from the 45° line. The ordinate distance from this line to a point occupied by an isotope, measured in terms of the number of neutrons, is the neutron excess or *isotopic number* corresponding to a particular value of Z. It is $I = N - Z$. We shall find (Chap. IX) that the stability line can be represented analytically by the approximate equation :

$$Z = \frac{A}{2 + 0 \cdot 0146 A^{2/3}} \tag{5.1}$$

where the symbols have their usual meaning. For example, writing $A = 64$, we find that Z is $28 \cdot 72 \backsimeq 29$. A reference to

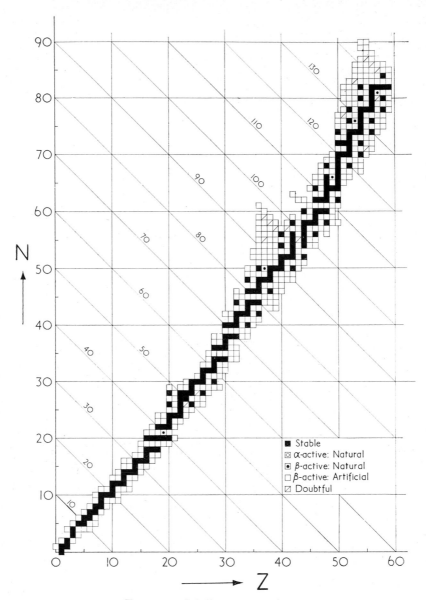

FIG. 5.1(a) *ZN* diagram : all nuclides.

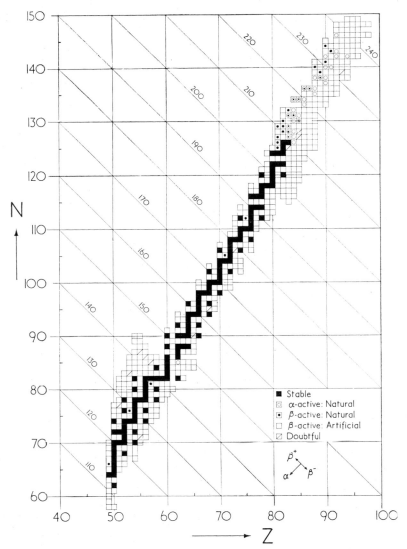

FIG. 5.1(b) *ZN* diagrams : all nuclides.

Fig. 5.1 shows that the isotope $^{64}_{29}$Cu, while unstable itself, lies between $^{63}_{29}$Cu and $^{65}_{29}$Cu and is therefore very close to the lowest region of the valley of stability.

On the two slopes of the valley of stability lie the unstable nuclides. They are divided by the valley into two classes. The "north-western slopes" are covered with negatron emitters— nuclides with an excess of neutrons. The "south-eastern slopes" are covered with positron emitters—nuclides deficient in neutrons.

Consider the nucleus ^A_ZX represented in Fig. 5.2, which is small part of the ZN diagram. It contains Z protons and $N(=A-Z)$ neutrons. The arrows indicate the displacement suffered by the nucleus for various types of disintegration, that is, the position of the daughter nucleus relative to its parent. For example, the emission of an α-particle changes ^A_ZX into some nucleus represented by $^{A-4}_{Z-2}$Y according to the reaction

$$^A_ZX \rightarrow ^{A-4}_{Z-2}Y + \alpha \quad (5.2)$$

The emission of a negatron means, as Fig. 5.2 shows, the transformation of a neutron into a proton :

$$^A_ZX \rightarrow ^{A}_{Z+1}Y + \beta^- \quad (5.3)$$

FIG. 5.2. Displacements of nuclide ^A_ZX for various types of transmutation.

The emission of a negatron thus changes the situation of the nucleus, moving it down the valley slope in what we have called the south-east direction into a position of lower potential energy, that is, closer to a position of stability. Similarly, positron emission moves a nucleus down the valley gradient in a north-west direction to a point nearer the line of stability.

Isomers

Another type of instability is instability to light quanta. A nucleus may continue for some time in an excited state and then revert from the higher energy level to the ground state with the

G H.N.S.

emission of a γ-ray. The mass number of the isotope is un-changed so that we have instances where one position in the ZN diagram is occupied by two isotopes which have the same nucleonic composition, the same mass number, but different nuclear energies. Such isotopes are called *isomers*.

It is convenient at this point to bring certain terms such as this, which are in common use, (Chap. I, p. 8) into relation with the ZN diagram. The following remarks should be read with Fig. 5.1 in mind.

(a) *Isotopes*. All isotopes ($Z =$ const.) lie on lines which are parallel to the N-axis.

(b) *Isotones*. These are nuclides of equal neutron number ($N =$ const.). Their loci are lines parallel to the Z-axis.

(c) *Isodiaphores* are nuclides of constant isotopic number ($I = N - Z =$ const.). Lines of constant isotopic number make an angle of 45° with the Z-axis.

(d) *Isobars* are nuclides of equal atomic mass number ($A = N + Z =$ const.).– They fall on lines which are inclined at an angle of 135° to the Z-axis (Fig. 5.1).

(e) *Isomers*, nuclides of identical composition and mass number but different internal energy might be represented by points on lines drawn normal to the ZN diagram. This involves a three-dimensional figure, the third axis being the energy axis.

It is clear from Fig. 5.2 that these five terms correspond to five types of nuclear instability :

	Type of Instability
(a) Isotopes	Neutron
(b) Isotones	Proton
(c) Isodiaphores	α-particle or deuteron
(d) Isobars	β-particle (+ or -),
	K-capture
(e) Isomers	γ-ray

The foregoing considerations emphasise the value of the ZN diagram for representing the relations between the isotopes and their various modes of transformation. The student will have realised, too, that the diagram, being the expression of the proton-neutron hypothesis of nuclear structure, also serves as a mnemonic in connection with the systematics of the nuclides.

In addition to the categories referred to above, the nuclides may be classified from the point of view of their degree of stability. They may be divided into three classes according to the lengths of their half-lives.

1. *Half-lives too short to be measured* (less than 10^{-8} second). These include nuclei in a very excited state which lose their excess energy and revert to a stable state by the emission of a γ-ray or by the ejection of a neutron or proton. Also included are certain nuclei in the ground state which are extremely unstable. An example is $^{8}_{4}Be$ which splits symmetrically into two α-particles.

2. *Measurable half-lives* (between 10^{-8} second and 10^{12} years). These include both the naturally radioactive elements which emit α-particles, β-particles and γ-rays and also most of the β-emitting nuclides ; also many isomers emitting γ-rays the half-lives of which vary from a small fraction of a second to several years.

3. *Half-lives too long to be measured* (more than 10^{12} years). If the half-life of a nuclide is very long, which is equivalent to saying that the relative number of particles emitted per second is very small, then the energy of the emitted particles will, by a known rule, be too small to be measured. This obviously suggests that elements now regarded as stable may yet be shown by new methods of augmented sensitivity to be feebly radioactive. Indeed, it is a plausible view-point that " stability " as used in this reference must be regarded as relative. Special methods have been developed in recent years by which half lives as short as 10^{-10} sec. or as long as 10^{17} years may be measured.

Isobars

As well as the empirical rules regarding isotopes which were set out in Chap. IV, there are further rules of comparable interest which may now be formulated. As an introduction a short digression into the topic of *isobars* will be helpful. The subject is more fully discussed in Chap. VIII.

Prior to 1913 it was thought that the chemical properties of an element were uniquely related to its atomic weight. Subsequently two discoveries showed that this view was incorrect. First, Aston proved that many elements were mixtures of atoms or molecules of different weights (isotopes) but all having identical chemical properties. Second, it was demonstrated that there existed pairs of nuclides of the same atomic weight—more strictly, the same atomic mass number—which had quite dissimilar chemical properties. These were named *isobares* by a British chemist, Stewart, in 1918. It became clear, therefore, that the chemical properties of an element are determined by the number of its circumnuclear electrons and that this number is related, not to the atomic weight, but to the atomic number of an element.

It is more important for the present purpose to note that the radioactive properties of a nuclide, associated as they are with the nucleus, are determined, not by the total mass of protons or neutrons, nor by both together (A), but by the relative numbers and arrangements of these nucleons. Isobaric nuclides contain the same total number of nucleons but the ratio of N/Z differs from one to another. Hence their nuclear properties differ, e.g., their rates of decay, if they are radioactive, are invariably different. An example is the *isobaric series*, RaB, RaC, RaC' and At. Each of these nuclei contains 214 nucleons but the relative numbers of protons and neutrons differ. Table 5.2 shows that their radioactive properties differ also.

TABLE 5.2

ISOBAR FAMILY $A = 214$

Nuclide	Number of :		Type of Radioactivity
	Protons	Neutrons	
RaB	82	132	β, 26·8 min.
RaC	83	131	β, 19·7 min.
RaC'	84	130	α, 145 sec.
At	85	129	α, very short

Many groups of isobaric nuclides exist ; they are recorded in the ZN diagram. The number of members of such groups varies from two to six or more. An example of such groups is the family of isobars of mass number 97 of which one member only is stable. The following representation is set down in a form which differentiates nuclides of even, from those of odd atomic number.

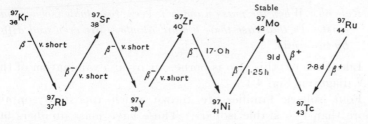

Further examples will be given in Chap. VIII where isobaric series are shown to lie transversely across the valley of stability. In the present instance eight members are located on two slopes of the valley in a plane normal to the line of stability. The ninth member ($^{97}_{42}$Mo) is at the lowest point of the valley. The nuclide at the highest elevation on the north-west slope is $^{97}_{36}$Kr which by five successive stages of negatron decay descends to the stable nuclide $^{97}_{42}$Mo. Similarly, $^{97}_{44}$Ru lies on the south-east slope and falls by two stages of positron disintegration also to become the only stable element of the series.

More Empirical Rules

Now, although there are many families of isobars if radio elements are included, the number of *stable* isobars is small. A survey of the ZN diagram of stable isotopes (Fig. 4.1) with reference to isobaric series leads to the formulation of further empirical rules in addition to those enunciated in the preceding chapter. These will now be stated.

The exceptions referred to in the following Rule are of interest ; they will be discussed in Chap. VIII.

Rule 6a. With three exceptions, when the mass number is odd, only one stable nuclide exists ; that is, there are no stable isobars of odd mass number.

The exceptions are the nuclides of mass numbers 113, 115, and 123.

We may interpret this Rule in terms of our figure of a valley of stability by supposing that at situations marked by odd mass numbers the gradients on both sides descend very steeply to the point where the solitary stable nucleus occupies the position of minimum potential energy.

Rule 6b. When the mass number is even, two stable isobars may exist. In that case their atomic numbers are even and differ by two units.

Like Rule 6a, this also is borne out by an examination of the ZN diagram (Fig. 4.1.)

Four isobaric families are known which appear to contain more than two stable isobars. These have mass numbers 96, 124, 130 and 136. To each of them correspond three apparently stable isobars of atomic numbers which, contrary to the Rule, differ by one unit. This anomaly will be referred to in the discussion of isobars in Chap. VIII.

Reverting to the valley of stability figure it may be supposed that, at points where the mass number A is even, the valley broadens at its lowest levels and allows two stable nuclides to occupy positions at approximately the same level of minimum energy. Since the atomic numbers differ by two units, the possibility of one of the nuclides being unstable with regard to the other is ruled out, for the transformation would involve the *simultaneous* emission of two negatrons or two positrons, an event which is in the highest degree improbable.

Rules 6a and 6b include an empirical isotope rule which was discussed by the Austrian physicist Mattauch in 1934. It may be formulated as follows :

Mattauch's Rule. There are no stable " adjacent " isobars, that is, isobars having atomic numbers which differ by unity.

It has been proved that apparent exceptions to this Rule are not valid. For instance, the isobaric series

$$\underset{18}{\overset{40}{}}A \qquad \underset{19}{\overset{40}{}}K \qquad \underset{20}{\overset{40}{}}Ca$$

consists of three elements which are found in the lithosphere and, if stable, they constitute an exception to Mattauch's rule. But the middle member, one of the rare odd-odd nuclides, has been shown to be unstable : $\underset{19}{\overset{40}{}}K$ is feebly radioactive, its half-life being about 190 million years. Other apparent exceptions are noted in Chap. VIII. The attempt to account qualitatively for these rules is also deferred to that chapter.

The " Magic Numbers "

We turn now to consider an isotope rule which has only recently emerged. The rule is important because of its direct bearing on hypotheses of nuclear structure. We have seen that some of the regularities which stand out in the ZN diagram might be interpreted by supposing that nucleons occur in pairs, each pair existing in a definite quantum state. A number of additional observations, including features of the ZN diagram, may be correlated, and in some sense explained, by supposing that paired nucleons are arranged in groups or " shells ". This notion is familiar to the chemist who thinks of the planetary electrons as being arranged in certain stable configurations. For example, atoms of helium, oxygen and argon with 2, 8 and 18 electrons respectively are exceptionally stable ; it is supposed that the electrons of these atoms constitute successive *closed shells*. If an atom contains one electron in excess or in defect of those of a closed shell, it is chemically active and has a strong affinity for an atom of any other element which has such a number of electrons that the combination of the two atoms results in a closed shell with its resulting stability. The 2, 8, 18... electrons of the successive shells are in different energy levels and it is becoming clearer that the notion of shells and energy levels, interpreted quantum mechanically, which has become familiar in atomic theory, may be applicable in suitably modified form to the atomic nucleus.

It has been found that nuclides containing certain definite numbers of nucleons of one kind are characterised by exceptional stability. Various lines of evidence lead to the same conclusion, that these numbers are significantly related to stages of nuclear build-up. No generally accepted theory exists which accounts for the empirical rule. It may be stated thus :

Rule 7. Nuclides having 2, 8, 20, 50, 82 *or* 126 *nucleons of the same kind are exceptionally stable.*

These numbers have been called the " magic numbers ". The topic is discussed in Chap. X, but while the ZN diagram is under consideration it is convenient to illustrate the Rule by reference to it. An examination of the diagram (Fig. 5.1) reveals the following interesting facts.

The average number of stable isotones for N even is just over three, but for $N = 20$ there are *five*, for $N = 50$ there are *six*, if we include $^{87}_{37}\text{Rb}$ which, although radioactive, has a very long half-life of about sixty thousand million years. For $N = 82$, there are *seven* stable isotones. Turning to isotopes, calcium $(Z = 20)$ has *five* isotopes widely spread, while tin $(Z = 50)$ has *ten*, more than any other nuclide. Finally, one of the most stable and most abundant in nature of all the nuclides, lead $(^{208}_{82}\text{Pb})$, has 82 protons and 126 neutrons.

The subject need not be developed here since it will be discussed later. It may be noted that this Rule, like the other isotope Rules so far stated, are to be read in relation to the ZN diagram. The next Rule, however, is to be inferred only from a more detailed isotopic chart in which a visual representation of the relative abundance of the isotopes is included.

A distinction to be borne in mind in relation to the meaning of isotopic " abundance " should be mentioned. There is the relative natural abundance of the elements and their isotopes in the earth, the sun and the stars. There is, on the other hand, the distribution of isotopic abundance in the mixture constituting a given element. It is the latter notion which is relevant here.

The distribution of isotopic abundance in the element molybdenum $(Z = 42)$ is shown in Table 5.3 which is due to Williams and Yuster (1946). The second column shows the number of atoms of each of the isotopes of the element *per* hundred atoms of $^{98}_{42}\text{Mo}$, the most abundant of the nine isotopes. The advantage of this method of representing natural abundance over the customary method of *percentage abundance* is that a correction of one of the figures, such as may result from improved measurements, does not affect the other figures. The percentage abundance of the isotopes of an element may vary from almost zero to one hundred per cent. Some of the ten isotopes of tin are present in an amount of less than one per cent, whereas gold has one isotope only. For nearly every element its isotopic composition is very accurately constant, that is to say, the relative abundance of its isotopes is independent of the source of the element. A few exceptions to this rule are noted in Chap. XII. The example of molybdenum serves

TABLE 5.3

RELATIVE ABUNDANCE OF ISOTOPES OF MOLYBDENUM

Mass Number	Relative Abundance	Percentage Abundance
92	66·6	15·8
93	—	—
94	38·0	9·0
95	66·1	15·7
96	69·5	16·6
97	39·8	9·5
98	100·0	23·8
99	—	—
100	40·5	9·6
		100·0

as an introduction to, and an illustration of the next isotope Rule.

Rule 8. The stable isotopes of an element of even atomic number Z, which have even values of the mass number A, are both more numerous and more abundant than are those having odd values of A.

Table 5.4 illustrates Rule 8 for even values of Z from 30 to 56. Among these fourteen elements there are 71 stable isotopes of even mass number and 22 of odd mass number. The contrast in the totals of percentage abundance is marked except in the case of $Z = 54$, a curious and unexplained anomaly.

This Rule is no doubt a consequence of the known superior stability of nuclides which contain an even number of nucleons over those containing an odd number.

The next isotope rule is also concerned with the relative abundance of the isotopes in the mixture which makes an element, but in this case it applies only to the heavier elements.

Rule 9. The lightest of the stable isotopes of any element of even atomic number, for $Z > 45$, has even mass number and, with four exceptions, its relative abundance is less than one per cent.

The percentage relative abundance of the lightest isotopes of stable elements of even atomic number exceeding 45 are given

TABLE 5.4

Z	Number of Isotopes		Total of Percentage Abundance	
	A even	A odd	A even	A odd
30	4	1	95·93	4·07
32	4	1	92·1	7·9
34	5	1	92·42	7·58
36	5	1	88·52	11·48
38	3	1	93·04	6·96
40	4	1	88·77	11·23
42	5	2	74·82	25·18
44	5	2	70·21	29·79
46	5	1	77·4	22·6
48	6	2	74·99	25·01
50	7	3	83·71	16·29
52	6	2	92·17	7·83
54	7	2	52·53	47·47
56	5	2	82·09	17·91
	71	22		

in Table 5.5 side by side with the corresponding figures of the heaviest isotopes for comparison. In the ZN diagram these lightest isotopes are in general the furthest removed from the stability line. According to one theory designed to explain the origin of the elements, the existence of these rare isotopes may indicate that at the time of the creation of the elements, there was an excess of neutrons, for without an excess of neutrons such elements would have been missing (Chap. XII).

The anomalous relative abundance of neodymium's $(Z = 60)$ lightest isotope is a striking feature of Table 5.5. The explanation of this curiosity is still to be found. Two relevant remarks may, however, be made. First, while the other isotopes which share the second column of Table 5.5 with neodymium are remote from the line of stability, the isotope $^{142}_{60}\text{Nd}$ is close to the energy minimum, that is, to the lowest part of the valley of stability. Second, the number of neutrons in this isotope is 82, a magic number. Magic numbers, we have seen, are associated with a special degree of stability.

TABLE 5.5

Z	Relative Abundance of	
	Lightest Isotope	Heaviest Isotope
	%	%
46	0·8	13·5
48	1·215	7·58
50	0·94	5·83
52	0·09	34·51
54	0·095	8·93
56	0·102	71·66
58	0·19	11·07
60	26·80	5·69
62	2·95	23·29
64	0·20	21·79
66	0·05	27·3
68	0·10	14·2
70	0·06	13·38
72	0·18	35·11
74	0·16	28·49
76	0·018	40·97
78	0·8	7·2
80	0·15	6·72
82	1·54	53·22

An isotope Rule of considerable interest, also concerned with relative abundance, is the following.

Rule 10a. When an isotope of odd mass number occurs between two adjacent isotopes, its abundance is always less than the sum of the abundance of the two isotopes.

The two adjacent isotopes will of course have even mass numbers. This rule has attracted attention because of the single exception to it. The isotope of xenon of mass number 129 fails to conform, as is evident from Table 5.6. So radical a departure from the Rule by one single trio only of the isotopes calls for an explanation. One of considerable interest is forthcoming. The anomaly of the high relative abundance of $^{129}_{54}$Xe has been attributed to the fact that it is the disintegration product of the radioactive isotope of iodine, $^{129}_{53}$I :

$$^{129}_{53}\text{I} \rightarrow {}^{129}_{54}\text{Xe} + \beta^- \qquad (5.4)$$

The half-life of $^{129}_{53}$I is long, more than 10^9 years, but this is short enough relative to the age of the earth to have produced since the earth was formed an accumulation of ^{129}Xe sufficient to make its abundance greater than the sum of the abundances of its two isotope neighbours. Indeed, this unique exception to Rule 10 has been used to make an estimate of the age of the elements.

A stricter form of Rule 10a is expressed in Rule 10b.

Rule 10b. Every isotope of odd mass number and even atomic number has at least one adjacent isotope of greater abundance.

In addition to the important exception to this Rule already noted there are two others, $^{149}_{62}$Sm and $^{195}_{78}$Pt. These, however, are not exceptions to Rule 10a. The relevant figures are given in Table 5.6.

TABLE 5.6

Element Z	Mass Number of Isotope A	Relative Abundance %
$_{54}$Xe	128	1·916
	129	26·23
	130	4·051
$_{62}$Sm	148	11·27
	149	13·84
	150	7·47
$_{78}$Pt	194	32·8
	195	33·7
	196	25·4

Natural Abundance of Elements

The next Rules are concerned with the relative abundance of the nuclides *in nature*. It is natural to anticipate that those elements of which the nuclear constitution is such that it makes for stability will be the most abundant in the crust of the earth. This proves to be the case. The even-even isotopes form the majority of the elements both in the earth and in meteorites. Elements of even atomic number are roughly 70 times more abundant than elements of odd atomic number.

Rule 11. *Nuclides which contain an even number of protons and an even number of neutrons are more abundant in nature than other species.*

This Rule is expressed in Table 5.7. There is one outstanding exception, viz., hydrogen. This element is very abundant in the stars. It will be realised that the accurate estimation of the relative abundance of the elements in nature is attended by considerable difficulties. None the less, sufficient information of a reliable nature has been forthcoming to establish the Rule. The subject is further discussed in Chap. XII (see Fig. 12.1).

Table 5.7 serves to establish the next Rule.

Rule 12. *Elements of atomic number from $Z = 1$ to $Z = 30$ are relatively abundant in nature. Elements of atomic number from $Z = 31$ to $Z = 92$ are of small, but constant abundance.*

The partition of the nuclides into two groups according to their natural abundance is seen to be remarkably clear-cut. The dividing line at $Z = 30$ is shown on a graph which displays log (abundance) *versus* atomic mass (Fig. 12.1). The explanation of the interesting phenomenon expressed in Rule 12 would appear to be connected in some way not properly understood with the mode of creation of the elements (Chap. XII).

The next Rule is concerned with the *natural abundance* of the members of isobaric pairs. It applies to nuclides of atomic number greater than 40. From Rules 6a and 6b it follows that it is concerned only with isotopes of even atomic number and even mass number, the atomic numbers of any of the isobaric pairs differing by two units.

To make a comparison between the natural abundance of two isotopes of different elements it is necessary to know (i) the relative abundance of the two elements and (ii) the fractions of the elements which consist of the isotopes concerned. The product of these two quantities is a basis for comparison of the natural abundance of the two isotopes of different atomic number. Consider an example. According to Table 5.7, for every 10^6 atoms of silicon found in nature, there are 28 atoms of molybdenum ($Z = 42$) and 15 atoms of ruthenium ($Z = 44$). Of the former 23·7 per cent is the isotope $^{98}_{42}Mo$ and of the latter 2·0 per cent is the isotope $^{98}_{44}Ru$ (Table 5.8). Hence 23·7 per

TABLE 5.7

RELATIVE ABUNDANCE OF THE ELEMENTS

Atoms per 10^4 Atoms of Silicon

Z	Element	Abundance	Z	Element	Abundance
1	H	$1 \cdot 25 \times 10^8$	44	Ru	0·15
2	He	$2 \cdot 78 \times 10^7$	45	Rh	0·057
3	Li	1	46	Pd	0·12
4	Be	0·2	47	Ag	0·043
5	B	0·2	48	Cd	0·10
6	C	30,000	49	In	0·011
7	N	80,000	50	Sn	0·96
8	O	160,000	51	Sb	0·021
9	F	10	52	Te	?
10	Ne	10,000	53	I	0·021
11	Na	462	54	Xe	?
12	Mg	8,870	55	Cs	0·010
13	Al	882	56	Ba	0·25
14	Si	10,000	57	La	0·021
15	P	170	58	Ce	0·023
16	S	3,300	59	Pr	0·0096
17	Cl	250	60	Nd	0·033
18	A	190	61	Pm	Unstable
19	K	69·3	62	Sm	0·012
20	Ca	670	63	Eu	0·0028
21	Sc	0·18	64	Gd	0·017
22	Ti	26·0	65	Tb	0·0052
23	V	3	66	Dy	0·02
24	Cr	93	67	Ho	0·0057
25	Mn	81	68	Er	0·016
26	Fe	26,200	69	Tm	0·0029
27	Co	157	70	Yb	0·015
28	Ni	2,130	71	Lu	0·0048
29	Cu	6·9	72	Hf	0·007
30	Zn	2·6	73	Ta	0·0032
31	Ga	0·54	74	W	0·19
32	Ge	0·39	75	Re	$6 \cdot 8 \times 10^{-5}(?)$
33	As	0·73	76	Os	0·057
34	Se	0·026	77	Ir	0·022
35	Br	0·042	78	Pt	0·14
36	Kr	?	79	Au	0·016
37	Rb	0·068	80	Hg	?
38	Sr	0·13	81	Tl	?
39	Y	0·097	82	Pb	0·43
40	Zr	1·42	83	Bi	0·0037
41	Cb	0·010	90	Th	0·011
42	Mo	0·28	92	U	0·0027
43	Tc	Unstable			

cent of $28 = 6 \cdot 63$ atoms of the element Mo is the isotope $^{98}_{42}\text{Mo}$ and $2 \cdot 0$ per cent of $15 = 0 \cdot 30$ atom of Ru is $^{98}_{44}\text{Ru}$. It follows that the ratio of the relative natural abundance of the isobar $A = 98$ of lower atomic number to that of higher atomic number

TABLE 5.8

1		2	3	4	5
Isobar		Atoms of Element (Z) per 10^6 Atoms Si	Isotope Abundance	Atoms of Isotope per 10^6 Atom Si $\times 100$	Ratio of Abundance of Isobars
Z	A		%		
40	92	142	17·1	2428	
42	92	28	15·8	442	5·5
40	94	142	17·4	2470	
42	94	28	9·1	255	9·7
42	96	28	16·5	462	
44	96	15	6·0	90	5·1
42	98	28	23·7	663	
44	98	15	2·0	30	22·1
42	100	28	9·6	269	
44	100	15	13·0	195	1·4
44	102	15	31·0	465	
46	102	12	0·8	10	46·5
44	104	15	18·0	270	
46	104	12	9·3	120	2·3
46	106	12	27·2	326	
48	106	10	1·2	12	27·1
46	108	12	26·8	322	
48	108	10	0·88	9	35·8
46	110	12	13·5	162	
48	110	10	12·3	123	1·3
48	112	10	24·0	240	
50	112	96	0·9	86	2·8
48	114	10	6·11	61	
50	114	96	4·61	443	(0·14)
48	116	10	18·7	187	
50	116	96	0·1	10	18·7
50	120				
52	120				
50	122				
52	122				

is 6·63/0·30 = 22·1, as shown in column 5 of Table 5.8. The comparison of the natural abundance of the members of pairs of isobars is shown in Table 5.8 and expressed in Rule 13.

NUCLEAR SPECIES

TABLE 5.8—*continued*

1		2	3	4	5
Isobar		Atoms of Element [Z] per 10^6 Atoms Si	Isotope Abundance	Atoms of Isotope per 10^6 Atom Si $\times 100$	Ratio of Abundance of Isobars
Z	A		%		
50	124				
52	124				
52	126				
54	126				
52	128				
54	128				
52	130				
54	130				
56	130				
54	132				
56	132				
54	134				
56	134				
54	136				
56	136	25	7·81	195	
58	136	2·3	0·19	0·4	487·5
56	138	25	71·6	1790	
58	138	2·3	0·25	5·8	309·0
58	142	2·3	11·0	25·3	
60	142	3·3	27·1	89·0	(0·28)
60	144	3·3	23·8	78	
62	144	1·2	3·1	3·7	21·1
60	148	3·3	5·7	18·0	
62	148	1·2	11·2	13·0	1·4
60	150	3·3	5·6	18·0	
62	150	1·2	7·4	9·0	2·0
62	152	1·2	26·6	32·0	
64	152	1·7	0·22	0·4	80
62	154	1·2	22·5	27·0	
64	154	1·7	2·1	3·6	7·5
64	156	1·7	20·6	35	
66	156	2	0·05	0·1	350
64	158	1·7	24·7	42	
66	158	2·0	0·09	0·18	233·0

TABLE 5.8—continued.

1	2	3	4	5
Isobar	Atoms of Element [Z] per 10^6 Atoms Si	Isotope Abundance	Atoms of Isotope per 10^6 Atom Si $\times 100$	Ratio of Abundance of Isobars
Z A		%		
64 160	1·7	21·7	37	
66 160	2·0	0·1	0·2	185·0
66 162	2·0	26·6	53	
68 162	1·6	0·1	0·16	331·3
66 164	2·0	27·3	55	
68 164	1·6	1·5	2·4	22·9
68 168	1·6	26·9	43	
70 168	1·5	0·14	0·2	215·0
68 170	1·6	14·2	23	
70 170	1·5	3·0	4·5	5·1
70 174	1·5	31·8	48	
72 174	0·7	0·18	0·126	381·0
70 176	1·5	12·7	19	
72 176	0·7	5·3	3·71	5·1
72 180	0·7	35·1	24·6	
74 180	19·0	0·13	2·5	10·8
74 184	19·0	30·6	581	
76 184	5·7	0·02	0·114	5096
74 186	19·0	28·4	540	
76 186	5·7	1·59	91	5·9
76 190	5·7	26·4	150	
78 190	14·0	0·006	0·084	1785·7
76 192	5·7	41·0	234	
78 192	14·0	0·78	11	21·3
78 196				
80 196				

Rule 13. *Of any pair of isobaric isotopes of atomic weight not less than 40 the member of lower atomic number is the more abundant ; the member of higher atomic number frequently exists in very small relative quantity.*

The first part of this Rule expresses the fact that the ratio in column 5 of Table 5.8 is greater than unity. There are only two exceptions. Evidence for the second part of the Rule is found

H

in column 4. The figures of the last column must not be regarded as anything more than an indication of the order of value of the abundance ratios. Their significance for the present discussion lies in the fact that, with only two exceptions, both of which are " magic " nuclei, they are greater than unity, indicating that the isobar of lower atomic number is almost invariably the more abundant of the two ; also, the high value of these ratios in many instances shows the very low relative abundance of many isobars of higher atomic number.

Rule 13 supports the hypothesis of the origin of the elements which supposes that the heavier elements were built up by the successive capture of neutrons by the lighter elements until neutron excess brought about a sequence of disintegrations by negatron emissions and terminated the building up process.

The thirteen isotope Rules set out in Chaps. IV and V, being empirical in character, serve as signposts pointing to some theory of nuclear structure adequate to account for them. In this lies their value. No doubt they have their intrinsic interest but their main value is to guide the theorist to a conception of the nucleus and nucleonic interactions from which the Rules may be simply and naturally deduced. This is a task of the future.

REFERENCE

Williams and Yuster, 1946, *Phys. Rev.*, **69**, 556.

CHAPTER VI

MASS DEFECT

In 1816 when the number of elements of which the atomic weights had been determined was few and the accuracy of the determinations relatively poor, an English physicist, William Prout, advanced the suggestion that greater accuracy in the measurements of the atomic weights might reveal that their values were *integral* multiples of that of hydrogen. The " protyle " of the early chemists, he suggested, might be hydrogen. Support for Prout's hypothesis was lacking for more than a century. Experiments of improved accuracy showed that the number of cases of atomic weights which were within five per cent of whole numbers was larger than could be accounted for by chance. On the other hand, there were conspicuous and puzzling exceptions ; many of the values were far from integers. A notorious example was chlorine which had an atomic weight of 35·457 on the chemists' scale 0 = 16.

This difficulty was decisively resolved in the twentieth century by the discovery of isotopes. It was then realised that Prout's hypothesis had indeed a valid foundation and that his choice of hydrogen as the building brick of the atom was more than an inspired guess. Aston, using the mass spectrograph which he built in 1919, showed that chlorine was a simple mixture of two species of atoms having masses which were very close to 35·000 and 37·000. There was no atom having a mass of 35·46. It was proved that chlorine gas was a mixture of atoms, approximately 75 per cent of them having atomic mass 35 and 25 per cent mass 37. The chemical balance was only able to determine the weight of many millions of mixed atoms, yielding a result of merely statistical significance ; while the mass spectrograph separated atoms of different masses and found both the mass and the relative abundance of each.

The results of the efforts of so many chemists in the nineteenth century to determine with ever closer approximation to accuracy the atomic weights of the elements might seem to have been deprived of any value, their methods having been superseded by the more accurate technique of the mass spectrograph. But one important fruit of these labours was now manifest. It had been demonstrated that, with certain significant exceptions which will be discussed in Chap. XII, the atomic weight of an element was independent of the source of the element. The inference is an important one : *the isotopic constitution of an element is constant.* In other words, the relative abundance of the isotopes in the mixture that constitutes a natural element does not vary with the place of origin of the element. Iron found in meteorites, for example, is a mixture of isotopes, the constituents of which are in the same relative proportions as those of iron found in the earth's crust.

Prout's hypothesis was accordingly replaced by Aston's *Whole Number Rule* which states that the weights of isotopes are expressible by numbers which are very nearly integral, fractional values of atomic weights being a consequence of the mixing of isotopes. " Very nearly integral " means here *within one per cent*—a much closer approximation to whole numbers than in the case of the chemists' atomic weights. As the difference between the latter and whole numbers proved to have significance, the deviation from integral values of the isotope masses has also found a meaningful explanation.

Table 6.1 is a list of the stable isotopes of the elements, together with the most stable isotopes of elements which have no stable isotopes. Stable isotopes not included in the list may exist but their relative abundance is so small that they have so far escaped detection. The Table shows that about three elements out of four consist of a mixture of two or more isotopes. Some elements are made up of many isotopes. Xenon, for example, has nine, tin has ten.

Atomic Weights

We have seen that the mass spectrograph is capable of measuring the masses of isotopes with an accuracy better than one part in 10^5, an achievement rarely equalled in the determination of atomic weights by chemical methods. It follows that the mass spectrograph affords in many instances the best means of measuring atomic weights. An example will make this clear.

TABLE 6.1

THE STABLE* ISOTOPES OF THE ELEMENTS

Z	Element	Mass number, A	Relative abundance, per cent	Isotope mass $O = 16 \cdot 0000$	Atomic weight, chemical scale (1940)
0	n	1		1·00895	
1	H	1	99·986	1·00813	1·0080
	(D)	2	0·014	2·01472	
2	He	3	10⁻⁶	3·01700	4·003
		4	100	4·00386	
3	Li	6	7·9	6·01692	6·940
		7	92·1	7·01816	
4	Be	9	100	9·01496	9·02
5	B	10	19·8	10·01617	10·82
		11	80·2	11·01290	
6	C	12	98·9	12·00388	12·010
		13	1·1	13·00756	
7	N	14	99·62	14·00753	14·008
		15	0·38	15·00487	
8	O	16	99·76	16·00000	16·0000
		17	0·14	17·00450	
		18	0·20	18·00485	
9	F	19	100	19·00447	19·00
10	Ne	20	90·00	19·99890	20·183
		21	0·27	20·99980	
		22	9·73	21·99862	
11	Na	23	100	22·99644	22·997
—12	Mg	24	77·4	23·9930	24·32
		25	11·5	24·9946	
		26	11·1	25·9901	
13	Al	27	100	26·9907	26·97
14	Si	28	89·6	27·9870	28·06
		29	6·2	28·9865	
		30	4·2	29·9839	
15	P	31	100	30·9844	30·98
16	S	32	95·04	31·9825	32·06
		33	0·74	32·9819	
		34	4·2	33·9798	
		36	0·016	?	
17	Cl	35	75·4	34·97884	35·470
		37	24·6	36·9777	
18	A	36	0·31	35·9973	39·944
		38	0·06	37·9746	
		40	99·63	39·9755	
19	K	39	93·44	38·976	39·096
		40	0·012	?	
		41	6·55	?	
20	Ca	40	96·96		40·08
		42	0·64		
		43	0·15		
		44	2·07		
		46	0·003		
		48	0·185		

* Including naturally occurring unstable isotopes.

THE STABLE* ISOTOPES OF THE ELEMENTS—*continued*

Z	Element	Mass number, A	Relative abundance, per cent	Isotope mass O = 16·0000	Atomic weight, chemical scale (1940)
21	Sc	45	100	44·96977	45·10
22	Ti	46	7·95		47·90
		47	7·75		
		48	73·45	47·966	
		49	5·51	48·964	
		50	5·34	49·963	
23	V	51	100		50·95
24	Cr	50	4·49		52·01
		52	83·78	51·959	
		53	9·43		
		54	2·30		
25	Mn	55	100		54·93
26	Fe	54	5·84	53·959	55·85
		56	91·68	55·957	
		57	2·17		
		58	0·31		
27	Co	59	100		58·94
28	Ni	58	67·4	57·9597	58·69
		60	26·7	59·949	
		61	1·2	60·9540	
		62	3·8	61·9496	
		64	0·88	63·9474	
29	Cu	63	68	62·957	63·57
		65	32	64·955	
30	Zn	64	50·9	63·957	65·38
		66	27·3	65·953	
		67	3·9		
		68	17·4	67·955	
		70	0·5	69·954	
31	Ga	69	61·5	68·956	69·72
		71	38·5	70·954	
32	Ge	70	21·2		72·60
		72	27·3		
		73	7·9		
		74	37·1		
		76	6·5		
33	As	75	100		74·91
34	Se	74	0·9		78·96
		76	9·5		
		77	8·3		
		78	24·0		
		80	48·0		
		82	9·3		
35	Br	79	50·6		79·916
		81	49·4		
36	Kr	78	0·35	77·945	83·7
		80	2·01		
		82	11·52	81·938	
		83	11·52		
		84	57·13	83·939	
		86	17·47	85·939	

THE STABLE* ISOTOPES OF THE ELEMENTS—*continued*

Z	Element	Mass number, A	Relative abundance, per cent	Isotope mass O=16·0000	Atomic weight, chemical scale (1940)
37	Rb	85	72·8		85·48
		87	27·2		
83	Sr	84	0·56		87·63
		86	9·86		
		87	7·02		
		88	82·56		
39	Y	89	100		88·92
40	Zr	90	48		91·22
		91	11·5		
		92	22		
		94	17		
		96	1·5		
41	Cb	93	100		92·91
42	Mo	92	14·9		95·95
		94	9·4	93·945	
		95	16·1	94·945	
		96	16·6	95·946	
		97	9·65	96·945	
		98	24·1	97·944	
		100	9·25	99·939	
43	Tc	99			
44	Ru	96	(5)	95·945	101·7
		98			
		99	(12)	98·944	
		100	(14)		
		101	(22)		
		102	(30)		
		104	(17)		
45	Rh	103	100	102·949	102·91
46	Pd	102	0·8		106·7
		104	9·3		
		105	22·6		
		106	27·2	105·946	
		108	26·8		
		110	13·5	109·944	
47	Ag	107	52·5	106·950	107·880
		109	47·5	108·949	
48	Cd	106	1·4		112·41
		108	1·0		
		110	12·8		
		111	13·0		
		112	24·2		
		113	12·3		
		114	28·0		
		116	7·3		
49	In	113	4·5		114·76
		115	95·5		

The Stable * Isotopes of the Elements—*continued*

Z	Element	Mass number, A	Relative abundance, per cent	Isotope mass O = 16·0000	Atomic weight, chemical scale (1940)
50	Sn	112	1·1		118·70
		114	1·8		
		115	0·4		
		116	15·5	115·943	
		117	19·1		
		118	22·5	117·940	
		119	9·8	118·938	
		120	28·5		
		122	5·5	121·946	
		124	6·8	123.945	
51	Sb	121	56		121·76
		123	44		
52	Te	122	2·9		127·61
		123	1·6		
		124	4·5		
		125	6·0		
		126	19·0		
		128	32·8		
		130	33·1		
53	I	127	100		126·92
54	Xe	124	0·094		131·3
		126	0·088		
		128	1·91		
		129	26·23	128·946	
		130	4·06		
		131	21·18		
		132	26·98	131·946	
		134	10·55		
		136	8·95		
55	Cs	133	100		132·91
56	Ba	130	0·101		137·36
		132	0·097		
		134	2·42		
		135	6·6		
		136	7·8		
		137	11·3		
		138	71·7		
57	La	139	100	138·955	138·92
58	Ce	136	Rare		140·13
		138	Rare		
		140	89		
		142	11		
59	Pr	141	100		140·92
60	Nd	142	25·95		144·27
		143	13·0		
		144	22·6		
		145	9·2		
		146	16·5	145·964	
		148	6·8	147·964	
		150	5·95	149·970	
61	Pm	147			

THE STABLE* ISOTOPES OF THE ELEMENTS—*continued*

Z	Element	Mass number, A	Relative abundance, per cent	Isotope mass O = 16·0000	Atomic weight, chemical scale (1940)
62	Sm	144	3		150·43
		147	17		
		148	14		
		149	15		
		150	5		
		152	26		
		154	20		
63	Eu	151	49		152·0
		153	51		
64	Gd	152	0·2		156·9
		154	1·5		
		155	21	154·977	
		156	22	155·977	
		157	17	156·976	
		158	22	157·976	
		160	16	159·976	
65	Tb	159	100		159·2
66	Dy	158	0·1		162·46
		160	1·5		
		161	22		
		162	24		
		163	24		
		164	28		
67	Ho	165	100		164·94
68	Er	162	0·25		167·2
		164	2		
		166	(35)		
		167	(24)		
		168	(29)		
		170	(10)		
69	Tm	169	100		169·4
70	Yb	168	0·06		173·04
		170	4·21		
		171	14·26		
		172	21·49		
		173	17·02		
		174	29·58		
		176	13·38		
71	Lu	175	97·5		174·99
		176	2·5		
72	Hf	174	(0·3)		178·6
		176	(5)		
		177	(19)		
		178	(28)		
		179	(18)		
		180	(30)		
73	Ta	181	100		180·88
74	W	180	0·2		183·92
		182	22·6		
		183	17·3		
		184	30·1		
		186	29·8		

THE STABLE* ISOTOPES OF THE ELEMENTS—*continued*

Z	Element	Mass number, A	Relative abundance, per cent	Isotope mass O = 16·0000	Atomic weight, chemical scale (1940)
75	Re	185	38·2		186·31
		187	61·8		
76	Os	184	0·018		190·2
		186	1·59		
		187	1·64		
		188	13·3		
		189	16·2		
		190	26·4	190·038	
		192	40·9	192·038	
77	Ir	191	38·5	191·038	193·1
		193	61·5	193·039	
78	Pt	192	0·8		195·23
		194	30·2	194·039	
		195	35·3	195·039	
		196	26·6	196·039	
		198	7·2	198·044	
79	Au	197	100	197·039	197·2
80	Hg	196	0·15		200·61
		198	10·12		
		199	17·04		
		200	23·25		
		201	13·18		
		202	29·54		
		204	6·72		
81	Tl	203	29·1	203·059	204·39
		205	70·9	205·059	
82	Pb	204	1·5	204·058	207·21
		206	23·6		
		207	22·6		
		208	52·3	208·057	
83	Bi	209	100	209·055	209·00
84	Po	210			
85	At	211			
86	Rn	222			222
87	Fr	223			
88	Ra	226			226·05
89	Ac	227			
90	Th	232	100		232·12
91	Pa	231			231
92	U	235	0·72		238·07
		238	99·28		

It must be noted in the first place that the chemists' scale and the physicists' scale of atomic weights are referred to two standards which differ. The physicists' standard is the mass of the *isotope* of oxygen, $^{16}_{8}O$, to which is attributed a value of 16 mass units. The chemist on the other hand takes the quotient : the weight of n atoms of *atmospheric oxygen* divided by n (where n is a very large number) to be 16. Since atmospheric oxygen contains three isotopes (see Table 6.2), the chemical scale and the physical scale are not identical. The difference is not large, neither is it negligible. The relation between them may be expressed thus :

Physical atomic weight = Chemical atomic weight × 1·000275.

TABLE 6.2

SOME ISOTOPIC WEIGHTS

Element	Mass Number	Isotopic Weight	Relative Abundance
		mu	%
Hydrogen	1	1·008123	99·98
	2	2·014708	0·02
Boron	10	10·01677	18·83
	11	11·01244	81·17
Carbon	12	12·00382	98·9
	13	13·00751	1·1
Nitrogen	14	14·00752	99·62
	15	15·00489	0·38
Oxygen	16	16·00000	99·76
	17	17·00450	0·04
	18	18·0049	0·20
Sulphur	32	31·9809	95·06
	33	32·9800	0·74
	34	33·9771	4·18
Chlorine	35	34·97867	75·4
	37	36·97750	24·6

The atomic weight of boron is an example of historic interest. From Table 6.2 it is seen that boron is a mixture of two isotopes : 18·83 per cent of $^{10}_{5}B$ and 81·17 per cent of $^{11}_{5}B$ of masses 10·01677 and 11·01244 respectively. This is equivalent on the chemical scale to an atomic weight of 10·822. Prior to the invention of the mass spectrograph the atomic weight of boron was listed by chemists as 10·90. Subsequent re-determinations of the atomic weight of boron by more sensitive chemical methods have established it at 10·82.

The superiority of the physical method of determining atomic weights depends on the sufficient accuracy of the figures representing (i) the mass of the isotope and (ii) its relative abundance. In the case of nitrogen, for example, both figures are known with considerable accuracy : v. Table 6.2. The atomic weight of nitrogen, which is found by chemical methods to be 14·008, can be calculated from these figures to a higher order of accuracy.

Mass Decrement and Mass Defect

It has been mentioned that the deviation of isotope masses from integral values is significant. It is related to the stability of the nucleus. It should be noted in passing, however, that " stability " is a relative term. It is not impossible that certain elements now listed as stable will prove, as the sensitivity of detecting instruments is improved, to be feebly radioactive with a correspondingly long half-life. At present a radioactive isotope with a half-life of more than 10^{12} years would in general emit particles of too low an energy for detection. Such elements must be regarded as stable until evidence to the contrary is forthcoming.

The difference between the mass of an isotope on the mass scale $^{16}_{8}O = 16$ and the nearest whole number is called the *mass decrement*. Obviously, the mass decrement of $^{16}_{8}O$ is zero. This is not to be confused with the *mass defect* which is referred to below. The mass decrement is not as significant physically as the mass defect. It was used by Aston in publishing the results of his mass spectrographic measurements. He made use in this reference of a quantity called the *packing fraction*.

If M is the mass of an isotope and the nearest integer to M is A (called the *mass number*), the mass decrement δ is defined as

$$\delta = M - A \qquad (6.1)$$

Then the packing fraction f is δ/A. Since A is the number of nucleons (protons + neutrons) in the nucleus, the packing fraction is the mass decrement per nucleon :

$$f = \frac{M - A}{A} \qquad (6.2)$$

We have seen that $M - A$ is always very small so that f is usually multiplied by 10^4 for convenience of tabulating. It may have either a positive or a negative value. For oxygen it is, by definition, zero.

Aston found that isotopes with mass numbers below $A = 19$ and above $A = 190$ have a positive packing fraction, whereas those with masses between $A = 19$ and $A = 190$ have a negative packing fraction. Fig. 6.1 shows Aston's original packing fraction curve.

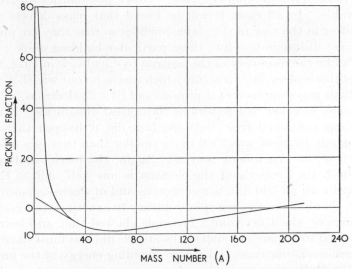

FIG. 6.1. Aston's original packing fraction curve (1927).

Reference to the packing fraction is made here partly as a matter of historical interest and partly because mass spectrograph measurements are often published as packing fractions. The mass decrement never exceeds 0·1 of a mass unit whereas the mass defect of the heavy elements is nearly 2 mass units.

In speaking of the mass " defect " of a nucleus we imply that its mass is less than the sum of the masses of its constituent parts in the free state, whatever the constituent parts may be. The mass defect is a measure of the stability of the nucleus. This is a consequence of Einstein's mass-energy relation $E = mc^2$ (Chap. VII). The mass defect may from this point of view be regarded as the work that must be done to pick the nucleus apart into the appropriate pieces and separate the components by distances at which their mutual interactions are negligible. It is evident, therefore, that the mass defect of an element will depend upon the nature of the building blocks of which the nucleus is assumed to be constructed. It may be supposed that nuclei are built from protons and electrons ; or, alternatively, having regard to the known stability of the α-particle, it may be assumed that a nucleus contains α-particles, protons and electrons. Other possibilities are conceivable. In all cases it will be found that mass defects are positive in the case of the stable nuclides so that they are proof against disintegration into these particular building units.

Before the discovery of the neutron by Chadwick in 1932, the hypothesis of nuclear structure which was in favour was that the nucleus was composed of A protons and $(A - Z)$ electrons. This scheme, however, led to serious theoretical difficulties. If the nucleus contained free electrons, how did it happen that its magnetic moment was 2000 times smaller than that of a single electron, as experiment proved? Again, the mechanical spin of both the proton and the electron is one half unit so that nuclei with an odd number of protons and of electrons (such as $^{15}_{8}O$) should have an even spin, contrary to experimental results. Moreover, the Uncertainty Principle showed that an electron confined to a space as small as the atomic nucleus must have an enormous momentum and a corresponding energy of the order of 100 MeV, an improbable value.

All these difficulties were resolved after the discovery of the neutron. Rutherford had suggested in 1920 the possibility of the existence of a neutral particle as a constituent of the nucleus (Rutherford, 1920). As soon as its existence was established experimentally, Heisenberg (1932) pointed out the great theoretical clarification that followed from using protons and neutrons as building blocks of the nucleus. The obvious difficulty that unneutralised protons exist in stable propinquity despite the Coulomb repulsion is met by supposing that nuclear attractive forces must exist between proton and neutron. It is supposed that protons and neutrons are different states of the same particle. They are therefore often referred to by the generic title *nucleons* to distinguish them from other particles, such as mesons, electrons etc., which are observed to issue from the nucleus.

The theory that the nucleus is built of Z protons and $N (= A - Z)$ neutrons is generally accepted today. In view of this, the term *mass defect* has assumed a definite meaning which may now be defined. Let a nucleus of mass m (in mass units on the scale $^{16}_8O = 16$) be made up of Z protons and N neutrons. The mass of the proton (m_p) and of the neutron (m_n) has been accurately measured :

$$m_p = 1 \cdot 007579 \text{ mu}$$
$$m_n = 1 \cdot 008938 \text{ mu} \qquad (6.3)$$
$$\text{(One mass unit} = 1 \cdot 6603 \times 10^{-24} \text{ gm.)}$$

The total mass W of these Z protons and N neutrons in the free state is

$$W = Zm_p + Nm_n \qquad (6.4)$$

The *mass defect* may now be defined as the difference between W, as calculated from Eq. (6.4) and m, as measured by the mass spectrograph, which, it should be remembered, measures *atomic* masses from which nuclear masses are deduced.

$$\text{Mass defect} = W - m \qquad (6.5)$$

The difference between this quantity and the mass decrement should be noted.

$$\text{Mass decrement} = W - A \qquad (6.6)$$

There is a certain amount of confusion of terminology in current textbooks between the two definitions. The relation (6.5) is of greater value since it affords a measure of the stability of the nucleus. If the nucleus is to hold together, $W - m$ must be a positive quantity ; the higher the value of the mass defect the greater is the stability of the nucleus. If $W - m$ were negative the nucleus must spontaneously disintegrate with evolution of energy.

We have seen that the original notion of mass defect is a general one and might be applied for example to the mass defect of a molecule considered to be built of atoms of known mass. Whereas, however, the mass defect of a nucleus is an appreciable fraction of the mass of the nucleus, molecular mass defects are negligibly small. It is to be noted in this connection that the mass defect of a nucleus as expressed in Eq. (6.5) can as well be written in terms of atomic masses. If M is the mass of an *atom* of atomic number Z and neutron number N and m_H is the mass of a hydrogen *atom*, we have

$$\text{mass defect} = W' - M \tag{6.7}$$

where $$W' = Zm_H + Nm_n \tag{6.8}$$

It is well known that the nucleus of the helium atom (the α-particle) is particularly stable. In comparison with the mass of this nucleus the mass defect is large, as a calculation will show. Since the α-particle contains 2 protons and 2 neutrons the mass of its constituents in the free state is

$$W' = 2m_H + 2m_n = 2(1 \cdot 008130) + 2(1 \cdot 00894)$$
$$= 4 \cdot 03414 \tag{6.9}$$

The mass of the helium atom as measured by the mass spectrograph is

$$M = 4 \cdot 00388 \tag{6.10}$$

Thus the mass defect is

$$W' - M = 0 \cdot 03026 \text{ mu} \tag{6.11}$$

This is equivalent in terms of energy to 28·2 MeV.

Let this be compared with the mass defect of the deuteron, the nucleus of the hydrogen isotope, deuterium. This nucleus is made up of 1 proton and 1 neutron, so that

$$W' = 1m_H + 1m_n = 2 \cdot 017070 \text{ mu} \tag{6.12}$$

and, since the experimentally determined mass of the deuteron is 2·014724, the mass defect is

$$W' - M = 0 \cdot 002346 \text{ mu} = 2 \cdot 18 \text{ MeV}. \tag{6.13}$$

Thus, whereas the mass defect per nucleon of the α-particle is 7·1 MeV. that of the deuteron is only 1·1 MeV. It follows that about six times as much work per nucleon would be required to pull an α-particle to pieces as would be necessary to separate the proton and neutron of a deuterium nucleus.

It is customary in compiling Tables of masses to tabulate *atomic* masses on a scale in which the arbitrarily chosen neutral atom $^{16}_8$O is given a mass of exactly 16 units. The unit in this case is called the *mass unit* (mu) and 1 mass unit is equivalent to 1·66 × 10^{-24} gm. or 931 MeV.

The mass defect of an *atom* is, strictly, made up of two parts corresponding to the binding energy of the nucleons and that of the circumnuclear electrons. The latter component, however, is small enough to be neglected. The binding energy of the electron which is removed from a neutral atom to make it a singly ionised particle is of the order of 10 electron volts. This is negligible since the rest mass of the electron itself is about half a million electron volts.

As will be seen in the next Chapter, the importance of nuclear mass and mass defect derives from its relation to the binding energy of the nucleus. The equivalence of mass and energy is the basis of this relationship. A mass of 1 gram is equivalent to 9·00 × 10^{20} ergs of energy. The mass of an electron pair can be completely transformed into kinetic energy. Rearrangement of the nucleons in a nucleus at a different energy level involves a change in mass of the nucleus. The importance for nuclear theory of devising means of measuring such changes in mass with high accuracy is obvious.

REFERENCES

W. Heisenberg, 1932, *Z. Physik*, **77**, 1.
E. Rutherford, 1920, *P.R.S.*, **97**, 374.

CHAPTER VII

BINDING ENERGY

THE amount of information which has been collected during the last three decades concerning the atomic nucleus is impressive. It is more than can be conveniently presented, even in summary, in a single volume and it is inevitable that future textbooks devoted to the physics of the atomic nucleus, if the treatment is not to be superficial, must be limited to topics which form the natural divisions of a very large subject. The present work being largely concerned with the results of high precision measurements of nuclear masses, it of necessity excludes many aspects of nuclear physics of comparable importance. This is a theme forming one of the natural divisions of the subject to which we referred in the Introduction. It leads quite naturally to a group of inter-related topics concerning the whole family of nuclides, their radii, mass defects, binding energies and relative abundances. Such a collection of cognate topics, when complete, has an organic unity. Its roots are in the data provided by the modern mass spectrograph and its fruits are insights into nuclear structure and energy.

Some information relating to nuclear forces is to be obtained from measurements of nuclear binding energies which are related to mass defects in a manner now to be explained. The *binding energy* of a nucleus, denoted here by the symbol BE, is the work that must be done to divide the nucleus into its constituent nucleons. Being a measure of the forces which cause the nucleons to cohere, it affords a quantitative estimate of the stability of the nucleus against total disintegration into protons and neutrons.

We have seen that when Z protons and N neutrons " condense " to form a stable nucleus it is not to be anticipated that the mass M of the nucleus will be given by $Zm_p + Nm_n$. The quantity M will be less than this by an amount which is defined as the mass defect. What has happened to this mass? It has been transformed into energy and the amount of this liberated energy is the measure of the binding energy of the nucleus. The equivalence of mass and energy was one of the remarkable consequences of Einstein's restricted theory of relativity published to a sceptical world in 1905. Its complete vindication in the realm of nuclear physics is one of the triumphs of relativity theory.

The mass-energy relation of Einstein is so fundamental in that area of nuclear physics which forms the subject matter of this book that it is worth while to devote some space to an examination of its theoretical basis. While this is not the place to discuss the topic as fully as its importance merits, it is appropriate to sketch in outline the arguments which show how Einstein's famous equation had its origin in the results of Michelson and Morley's classical measurement of the velocity of light. The reader who requires a fuller and more detailed discussion is referred to the many lucid accounts of relativity theory now available.

Equivalence of Mass and Energy

The wave theory of light was developed on the assumption of the existence of an all-pervading, luminiferous ether. It was held that, if this problematical entity had real existence, it was unlikely to be stationary relative to the earth or to the solar system. It should accordingly be possible to measure the speed of the earth relative to the ether v by observations of the velocity of light c.

Suppose, first, that a beam of light travels *parallel* to the earth's motion through the ether for a distance l and is then reflected by a mirror back along the same path. The time occupied by the double journey is

$$\frac{l}{c+v} + \frac{l}{c-v} = \frac{2lc}{c^2 - v^2} \tag{7.1}$$

Now suppose that the beam of light travels perpendicular to the earth's motion through the ether to a mirror M (Fig. 7.1), situated at the same distance l from the source, and back again. The path length is no longer equal to $2l$. It is easy to prove

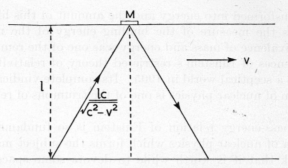

FIG. 7.1. The Michelson Morley experiment.

that it is $2lc/\sqrt{c^2 - v^2}$. Hence the time occupied in this case is $2l\sqrt{c^2 - v^2}$ and from Eq. (7.1)

$$\text{ratio of the times} = 1/\sqrt{1 - v^2/c^2} \qquad (7.2)$$

Hence it was proved that the effect should be easily detected by the displacement of interference fringes produced by an interferometer.

An experiment having a high degree of reliability was undertaken in 1881 by A. A. Michelson to test the validity of the foregoing theory. It was repeated with every possible refinement in 1887 by Michelson and Morley and the outcome made physics history. The results were negative. *The velocity v proved to be zero.* The scientific dilemma was acute.

In 1893, G. F. FitzGerald suggested that the ether hypothesis might be retained and at the same time the Michelson Morley result explained if it were assumed that all bodies moving parallel to the earth's motion relative to the ether suffered a contraction of length by a factor $\sqrt{1 - v^2/c^2}$, the denominator of Eq. (7.2). The FitzGerald suggestion, although unconfirmed in its simple form, bore fruit. Einstein, on the basis of rigid incontrovertible argument from first principles, showed that the contraction was an "appearance" resulting from relative motion. The difficulty of understanding Einstein's theory in its early presentation became notorious but it originated not so much in its intrinsic complexity as in the methods of its exposition. In anticipation of Einstein's rigorous deductions, a Dutch physicist, H. A. Lorentz, had shown that one of the

consequences of the " Fitzgerald contraction " was that the
mass of a particle would increase as its velocity approached
asymptotically that of light. The argument may be presented
in an elementary manner as follows.

Sir J. J. Thomson had in 1881 derived an equation based on
the fact that a particle carrying an electric charge, since its
motion produced a magnetic field, must have electromagnetic
mass. If it be assumed that the mass m of an electron (taken
as spherical) of radius r and electric charge e is entirely electromagnetic, then, for moderate velocities, as Thomson showed,

$$r = 2e^2/3m \qquad (7.3)$$

(e is measured in electromagnetic units).

Now, Lorentz argued that if r_0 is the radius of an electron at
rest, its radius r when moving with a velocity v would be less by
the Fitzgerald factor :

$$r = r_0\sqrt{1 - v^2/c^2} \qquad (7.4)$$

Since from Eq. (7.3) the mass of an electron should be inversely
proportional to its radius, if m_0 is the *rest-mass* of the electron
and m its mass when moving with velocity v,

$$m/m_0 = r_0/r = 1/\sqrt{1 - v^2/c^2}$$
or $$m = m_0/\sqrt{1 - v^2/c^2} \qquad (7.5)$$

This equation, which has been verified by many and diverse
experiments, is one of the trophies of relativity theory. The
arguments by which it was derived were far from adequate until
Einstein demonstrated it as one of the consequences of his
theory. Eq. (7.5) shows that the " relativistic mass " of a
particle increases very rapidly when its velocity exceeds about
$0.95\ c$. For instance, if $v/c = 0.99$ the mass of the particle is
more than seven times its rest-mass (Fig. 0.1, p. xvii).

The last step in the derivation of the mass-energy equation
requires only elementary mechanics and algebra. When a
force F acting on a body moves it through a distance dx, the
increase of the kinetic energy dE is given by

$$dE = F \cdot dx \qquad (7.6)$$

But, by Newton's second law of motion, $F = d(mv)/dt$ so that

$$dE = F \cdot dx = d(mv) \cdot \frac{dx}{dt} = v\,d(mv)$$

that is,

$$dE = v^2\,dm + mv\,dv \qquad (7.7)$$

Eq. 7.5 may be written

$$m^2(c^2 - v^2) = m_0^2 c^2 \qquad (7.8)$$

Differentiating this, noting that c and m_0 are constant,

$$(c^2 - v^2)\,dm - mv\,dv = 0 \qquad (7.9)$$

Comparing this with Eq. (7.7), we find

$$dE = dm \cdot c^2 \qquad (7.10)$$

This is one form of the mass-energy relation.

In the foregoing argument the energy was kinetic energy, but Einstein showed that, no matter what form the energy E may take, the mass of the body will increase by an amount E/c^2 so that, quite generally

$$E = mc^2 \qquad (7.11)$$

For example, a hot body has greater mass than the same body when cold. Care must be taken when applying Eq. (7.11) to employ the appropriate units. If m is in grams and c in centimetres per second, then E is in ergs. If m is in kilograms and c in metres per second, E is in joules.

Various units are employed in connection with nuclear mass and energy. They include (a) the *gram*, (b) the *mass unit*, (c) the *erg*, (d) the *calorie*, (e) the *electron volt* and (f) the *kilowatt hour*. The conversion factors are set out in Appendix I. One of the most useful of these relations is

1 mu (mass unit) = 931 MeV (million electron volts).

The quantities of energy involved in nuclear reactions per unit mass are very much larger than those involved in chemical reactions. It is well known that to remove its electron from a hydrogen atom requires an expenditure of energy of 13·5 electron volts. On the other hand, to remove a neutron from the nucleus of $^{21}_{10}\mathrm{Ne}$ demands 6,600,000 electron volts. The total binding energy of all the electrons of the heaviest atom is small relative to the binding energy of a single nucleon.

As we have said, the equivalence of mass and energy expressed in Eq. (7.11) is quite general. The reason why it does not figure in macrophysics is that the quantities involved are too small to be measured. For example, if a litre of water is raised in temperature from freezing point to boiling point, the 10^5 calories added to the water represent an addition of mass. The amount of this increase may be easily calculated. Since 10^5 calories is equivalent to $4\cdot18 \times 10^{12}$ ergs (Appendix Ib), we have by substituting in Eq. (7.11)

$$4\cdot18 \times 10^{12} = m \times (3 \times 10^{10})^2$$

whence $\qquad\qquad m = 4\cdot6 \times 10^{-9}$ gm.

This mass is too small to measure by macroscopic methods and the percentage change in relation to the thousand grams of water is still less appreciable.

On the other hand the percentage change of mass in nuclear reactions is relatively large. The fusion of four hydrogen nuclei into an α-particle would involve a large liberation of energy. Taking the total mass of four hydrogen atoms as $4 \times 1\cdot008130 = 4\cdot0325$ mu and the mass of the helium atom as $4\cdot00388$, the difference, $0\cdot02864$ mu represents a loss of mass of about $0\cdot7$ per cent.

Stability

The binding energy (BE) of a nucleus is a measure of its stability against complete disintegration. If the binding energy (essentially a negative quantity) is large, the nucleus is relatively stable since much energy must be added to it in order to resolve it completely into its constituent nucleons. If the binding energy is zero, the equilibrium of the nucleus is unstable. A positive binding energy means that the nucleus cannot have more than momentary existence.

To illustrate this relation between the binding energy and stability of a nucleus, let us consider four possible combinations of 4 protons and 4 neutrons into not more than two nuclei, noting the total BE of each group. This is calculated from the mass defect from the total mass of 4 protons *plus* 4 neutrons.

It is evident from the last column of this Table that *in respect of complete disintegration into* 8 *nucleons* the α-particles have

TABLE 7.1

Nuclei	Binding Energy (MeV)		
		Total	per Nucleon
1. $^4_2$He	28·18		7·045
$^4_2$He	28·18	56·36	7·045
2. $^8_4$Be	56·28	56·28	7·035
3. $^5_2$He	27·26		5·452
$^3_2$He	7·63	34·89	2·543
4. $^6_3$Li	31·89		5·315
$^2_1$H	2·19	34·08	1·095

superior stability in comparison with the other nuclei. Next to this stands $^8_4$Be. But this, in fact, is unstable. The reason for this is that, while it is true that energy of the value of 56·28 MeV would be required to disperse completely the 8 nucleons of $^8_4$Be, its division into two α-particles requires no expenditure of energy. Indeed, this process is exothermic with the evolution of 0·8 (= 56·36 − 56·28) MeV of energy. It therefore proceeds spontaneously. In the same way the third pair of nuclei appears to be more stable than the fourth but this again is in respect of complete disintegration into 8 nucleons. In fact, $^5_2$He is unstable to neutron decay :

$$^5_2\text{He} \rightarrow {}^4_2\text{He} + n$$

The *BE* figures show that this reaction, too, proceeds spontaneously.

It is important to grasp the implication of these results. The binding energy of a nucleus, in the customary meaning of the term, has reference to its total dissociation into its component nucleons. But when we consider the stability of a nucleus, we must enquire : stability against what? Against β-decay? Against neutron decay? Against fission? Against resolution into its constituent protons and neutrons? To obtain a valid answer to the question of nuclear stability we must accordingly determine its binding energy in respect of all possible modes of subdividing it. If in relation to a particular mode of subdivision the nucleus has a negative binding energy,

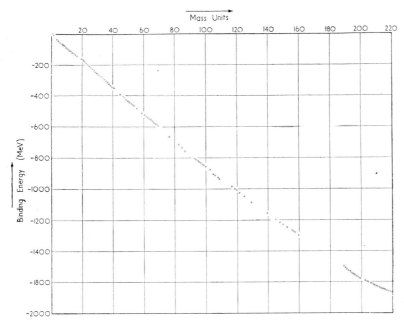

FIG. 7.2. Binding energy of stable nuclides *v*. mass number.

that mode of division is improbable : the nucleus is stable against disintegration in that particular way. If, on the other hand, the binding energy has a positive value in respect of any mode of division whatever, its decay is inevitable and will proceed in that mode with the evolution of energy. In such a case the nucleus can have only temporary existence. We may therefore conclude that all nuclides called " stable " are stable against disintegration in any manner whatever. Nevertheless, the degree of stability is relative. It is not a fixed quantity but varies with the possible methods of subdivision.

The binding energy of stable nuclides plotted against their mass numbers is shown in Fig. 7.2. From this graph an important conclusion may be drawn. From $A = 20$ to $A = 160$ there is a near-linear relation between BE and A, the ratio BE/A being about 8·5. Hence, for this range of atomic mass, the average binding energy per nucleon $(\bar{B})$ is constant and equal to about 8·5 MeV. For values of A above 160, the value of $\bar{B}$ falls only slowly, its mean value being about 7·8 MeV per nucleon.

In Fig. 7·3 $\bar{B}$ is plotted against A. It will be noticed that the curve is irregular until A exceeds 20, that there is a long stretch for which $\bar{B}$ is higher and nearly constant at 8·5 MeV per

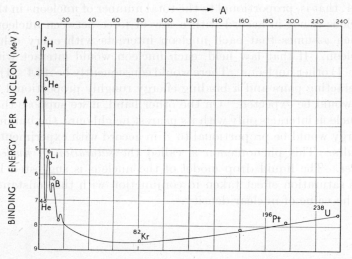

FIG. 7.3. Variation of binding energy per nucleon with mass number.

nucleon, and that for high mass numbers $\bar{B}$ is lower, pointing to a decrease in stability against complete disintegration. The maximum value of the binding energy occurs in the vicinity of the transition elements, iron, nickel and cobalt.

The curve of Fig. 7·3 shows that certain nuclei, among them ^{4}He, ^{12}C and ^{16}O have higher values of $\bar{B}$ than have their neighbouring nuclides. This is often interpreted as implying that such nuclei have α-particles as constituents. It is to be considered in relation to the fact that nuclei containing even numbers of protons and neutrons have superior stability. It is significant that the binding energy of a nucleon attached to a light element which might contain a completed number of α-particles is small. Thus, the neutron which is added to $^{12}_{6}$C to form $^{13}_{6}$C is bound with an energy of only 4·89 MeV. It is not possible to add a neutron to $^{4}_{2}$He to form $^{5}_{2}$He because the binding energy would be positive. The same difficulty of adding a proton to $^{4}_{2}$He accounts for the non-existence of the nuclide $^{5}_{3}$Li. It may be noted, however, that the addition of a neutron to $^{8}_{4}$Be produces the only stable isotope of beryllium. On the other hand, there is a substantial liberation of energy when a proton is added to $^{7}_{3}$Li to form $^{8}_{4}$Be.

The fact that the binding energy of a nucleus is proportional to A, that is, proportional to the total number of nucleons in the nucleus is not in accord with a law of force between nucleons which assumes that each nucleon interacts with every other nucleon. If that law held, each nucleon would interact with $(A-1)$ other nucleons. There would consequently be $A(A-1)/2$ interacting pairs and a binding energy roughly proportional to A^2 would be expected. On the other hand, if we suppose that a nucleon interacts only with its nearest neighbours, the binding energy would be proportional to A in accord with experimental results. This phenomenon is called the *saturation of nuclear forces*. The liquid drop model of the nucleus is suggested by this saturation effect taken in conjunction with the constancy of the value of nuclear density.

CHAPTER VIII

ISOBARS

THE remarkable regularities among the elements in respect of their chemical properties which is made evident by the periodic classification of Mayer and Mendelejeff (1869) led, as we have seen, to the belief by chemists that the chemical properties of the elements were directly related to their atomic weights, for it was upon these weights that the periodic system was based. In 1913, however, Moseley's investigation of the X-ray spectra of the elements, together with the discovery of isotopes, showed that it was the *atomic number* (Z) of an element, not its atomic weight, which was correlated with the chemical properties of an element. The atomic number is the basic property of the atom ; the atomic weight is incidental. Cases came to light of elements of almost identical atomic weight which had differing chemical and physical properties. Radium B $(Z = 82)$, Radium C $(Z = 83)$ and Radium C' $(Z = 84)$, having the same mass number $(A = 214)$ and approximately the same atomic weights, differ in chemical and radioactive properties.

Nuclides such as these, which have the same mass number and different atomic numbers, are called *isobars* (Greek, ισος, equal βαρος, weight). The name was suggested by Stewart (1918), a British chemist, who called them " isobares ", the term *isobars* having been bespoken by the meteorologists to designate cartographic lines of equal atmospheric pressure. The term *isobars*, however, is now universally used also by nuclear physicists.

The discoveries of the last three decades have made it clear that the properties of an element may be related either to the planetary electrons of the atom or to its nucleus or to both simultaneously. (i) The chemical properties of an element as well as its optical and X-ray spectra are explained by reference to circumnuclear electrons, the number of which is the atomic number of the element. Thus, the isotopes of a given element

119

will have, with certain minor differences, identical chemical and optical properties. (ii) The behaviour of an ionised atom in an electric or magnetic field depends both on its deficiency in electrons and also on the number of nucleons (A) in its nucleus. (iii) On the other hand, the radioactive properties of an element are associated exclusively with the nucleus, depending on the relative numbers of protons and neutrons in the nucleus.

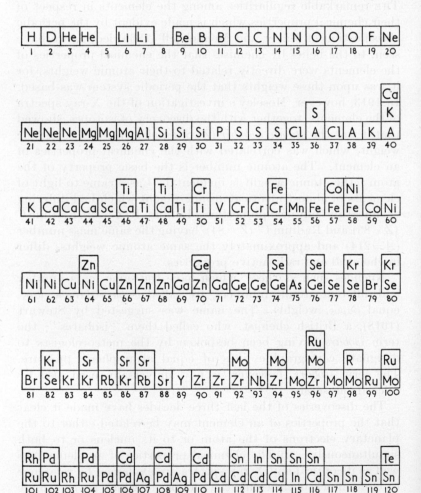

FIG. 8.1a. Isobars.

These considerations serve to emphasise again the value of the ZN diagram in relation to the subject matter of this book. The diagram represents, for every known nuclide, both the number of circumnuclear electrons (Z), on which the chemical and optical properties of the nuclide depend, and the number and relative proportions of protons (Z) and neutrons (N) which determine the radioactive properties of the nuclide. It shows

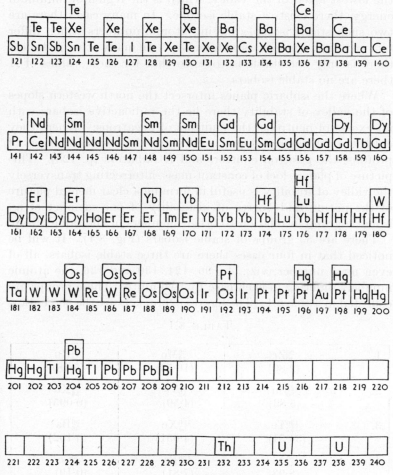

FIG. 8.1b. Isobars.

at a glance the families of isotopes, $Z =$ constant, and the family of isotones, $N =$ constant. It shows also the isobaric groups, $Z + N =$ constant. We have noted that the last equation represents lines on the ZN diagram which have a negative gradient (Fig. 5.1). These parallel lines, the isobaric lines, corresponding to each of which there is a definite value of A, $(= Z + N)$, cut the valley of stability transversely (Chap. V, p. 81). In the place where an isobaric line or plane intersects the lowest levels of the valley, which is the region of minimum energy, there exists a stable isotope. In many cases there are two such stable isotopes having atomic numbers which differ by two units : these are stable isobars. In many other instances there is only one stable isotope, so that for these values of A there are no stable isobars.

Where the isobaric planes intersect the north-western slopes of the valley of stability there lie the radioactive isobars with an excess of neutrons, the emitters of negatrons. Where they cut the south-eastern slopes are situated those with an excess of protons, the positron emitters and K-radiators (p. 128). This picture of planes, loci of constant mass, intersecting transversely the valley of stability is useful in forming a clear mental picture of the nature and degree of instability of one member of an isobaric group in relation to other members of the same group.

There are 53 groups of stable isobars (Fig. 8.1). It will be noticed that in four cases there are three stable isobars, all of even mass number, viz., $A = 96$, 124, 130 and 136, the atomic numbers differing in each case by two units. These groups are collected in Table 8.1. The figures in brackets are the percentage

TABLE 8.1

1.	$^{96}_{40}$Zr	$^{96}_{42}$Mo	$^{96}_{44}$Ru
	(2·80)	(16·53)	(5·68)
2.	$^{124}_{50}$Sn	$^{124}_{52}$Te	$^{124}_{54}$Xe
	(5·83)	(4·59)	(0·095)
3.	$^{130}_{52}$Te	$^{130}_{54}$Xe	$^{130}_{56}$Ba
	(34·51)	(4·051)	(0·102)
4.	$^{136}_{54}$Xe	$^{136}_{56}$Ba	$^{136}_{58}$Ce
	(8·93)	(7·81)	(0·19)

abundance of the isotope relative, not to the other two members of the isobaric group, but to other isotopes of the same element.

There are four other cases which occur in nature. In these the atomic numbers differ by unity and the middle member of each isobaric triplet is an odd-odd nuclide. These groups are collected in Table 8.2.

TABLE 8.2

5.	$^{40}_{18}A\,(i=0)$ (99·57)	$^{40}_{19}K\,(i=4)$ (0·011)	$^{40}_{20}Ca\,(i=0)$ (96·92)
6.	$^{50}_{22}Ti$ (5·34)	$^{50}_{23}V$ (v. small)	$^{50}_{24}Cr$ (4·31)
7.	$^{138}_{56}Ba$ (71·66)	$^{138}_{57}La$ (0·089)	$^{138}_{58}Ce$ (0·25)
8.	$^{176}_{70}Yb$ (13·38)	$^{176}_{71}Lu$ (2·5)	$^{176}_{72}Hf$ (5·30)

Of these twelve nuclides the middle member of groups 5 and 8 are known to be radioactive. The activity is feeble and the half-life is long. The isotope ^{40}K decays by negatron emission ; positron emission has not been observed. The half-life of ^{40}K is about $0 \cdot 19 \times 10^9$ years, that of $^{176}_{71}Lu$ is about $2 \cdot 4 \times 10^{10}$ years. The relative abundance of $^{40}_{19}K$ is about 1 part per 1000 parts of potassium. The relative abundance of $^{50}_{23}V$ and of $^{138}_{57}La$ is very small and it is probable that both these nuclides are radioactive species of very long half-lives, the activity being too feeble to be detected. The protracted half-lives are associated with the large change of spin (i) involved in the disintegration.

Binding Energies

These examples serve to stimulate study of the connection between electron emission and the differences of binding energies between isobars. We shall see that an understanding of the relation between the masses of isobars and β-decay which accompanies the transformation of one isobar into another provides a clue to the explanation of the rules governing the occurrence and non-occurrence of stable isobars. The three possible cases are : (i) emission of a β^--particle, (ii) emission of a β^+-particle and (iii) K-capture. It is to be noted that the binding energies of circumnuclear electrons are neglected in comparison with the very much greater nuclear binding energies.

(i) *Negatron emission.* The energy changes may be summarised as follows. The atom at rest, of mass $_zM$, loses the kinetic energies of the emitted negatron and neutrino and gains recoil energy. Let the net value of this disintegration energy be ΔE. The new atom of mass $_{z+1}M$ gains a free electron which has a rest mass of m_0. Expressing the rest masses of the original system in the relativistic form $(_zM + m_0)c^2$ and that of the final system as $(_{z+1}M + m_0)c^2$, we have, since mass-energy is conserved,

$$(_zM + m_0)c^2 = \Delta E + (_{z+1}M + m_0)c^2$$

or $$\Delta E = (_zM - _{z+1}M)c^2 \qquad (8.1)$$

(ii) *Positron emission.* The original system consists simply of an atom at rest, its total energy being $_zMc^2$. The kinetic energies involved are : (*a*) that of the ejected positron, (*b*) that of the recoil of the nucleus and (*c*) the removal of a circumnuclear electron (zero energy) to restore electrical neutrality. Let the total value of this energy be ΔE. A positron and a negatron have been removed from the original atom, so that the mass-energy balance is

$$_zMc^2 = (_{z-1}M + 2m_0)c^2 + \Delta E$$

or $$\Delta E = (_zM - _{z-1}M - 2m_0)c^2 \qquad (8.2)$$

(iii) *K-capture.* In this case, where a circumnuclear electron is captured by the nucleus, no kinetic energy is involved. But the electrons in rearranging their positions emit X-rays which are characteristic not of the parent, but of the daughter nucleus. If the energy of the X-rays be ΔE,

$$_zMc^2 = _{z-1}Mc^2 + \Delta E$$

or $$\Delta E = (_zM - _{z-1}M)c^2 \qquad (8.3)$$

In these three processes the parent and daughter nuclides are adjacent isobars ; they have the same mass numbers and their atomic numbers differ by unity. Can they both be stable?

The criterion of negatron emission is, from Eq. (8.1),

$$_zM > _{z+1}M \ ;$$

that of positron emission is, from Eq. (8.2),

$$_ZM > _{Z-1}M + 2m_0 \; ;$$

and that of K-capture is, from Eq. (8.3),

$$_ZM > _{Z-1}M$$

From these inequalities it is evident that, if there be any excess of mass, however slight, of $_ZM$ over $_{Z+1}M$, negatron emission must occur and stable adjacent isobars cannot co-exist. Positron emission will occur if $_{Z+1}M$ exceeds $_ZM$ by $2m_0$. The energy available for K-capture exceeds that for positron emission by $2m_0$.

These considerations of energy balance assist us in under-standing why there are as few as three pairs of *adjacent* stable isobars in nature—and the stability of one of the partners is in each case very doubtful—whereas there are more than fifty cases of natural stable isobars which are not adjacent, their atomic numbers differing by two units. The three pairs re-ferred to are shown in Table 8.3. The figures of relative abundance denote the abundance of the isotope relative to other isotopes in the same family.

TABLE 8.3

ADJACENT ISOBARS

Isobars		Relative Abundance		Spin(i)	
$^{113}_{48}Cd$		12·26		$\frac{1}{2}$	
	$^{113}_{49}In$		4·23		$\frac{9}{2}$
$^{115}_{49}In$		95·66		$\frac{9}{2}$	
	$^{115}_{50}Sn$		0·33		$\frac{1}{2}$
$^{123}_{51}Sb$		42·72		$\frac{9}{2}$	
	$^{123}_{52}Te$		0·85		?

The instability of one member of the first pair with respect to the other is affected by the spin change involved in a trans-formation. This is large ($\Delta i = 8/2$) so that there would be a highly forbidden transition and a correspondingly long half-life. The same remark applies also to the second case (Metzer and

K   H.N.S.

Deutsch, 1948). The spin of $^{123}_{52}$Te is unknown. It may be significant, too, that the atomic number of each of these nuclides is close to 50, which is known to be a configuration of unusual stability.

The disintegration of none of these elements in the ground state has been observed. The low relative abundance of the member of each pair which has the higher atomic number suggests that any decay process may be one of K-capture, e.g.,

$$^{115}_{50}\text{Sn} \xrightarrow{K\text{-capture}} {}^{115}_{49}\text{In}$$

It was observed by Bell, Ketelle and Cassidy, however, that the isomer of $^{115}_{49}$In, written $^{115}_{49}$In*, decays in two ways, one by normal isomeric transition to the ground state and the other by beta decay, to form $^{115}_{50}$Sn. The half-life is 4·5 hours in each case. Now the spin of $^{115}_{50}$Sn is $\frac{1}{2}$, and the spin of $^{115}_{49}$In is $\frac{9}{2}$ in the ground state and $\frac{1}{2}$ in the excited state. So the disintegration

$$^{115}_{49}\text{In}^* \xrightarrow{\quad \beta^- \quad} {}^{115}_{50}\text{Sn}$$

involving no change of spin, is permitted.

There are found in nature two cases of pairs of adjacent isobars in which one member of the pair is unstable with respect to the other. One of these, the rubidium-strontium pair, has been carefully studied. It was found that a mineral containing rubidium contained also a small quantity of the $^{87}_{38}$Sr isotope of strontium *with no other strontium isotope.* This is readily accounted for by the feeble radioactivity of $^{87}_{37}$Rb :

$$^{87}_{37}\text{Rb} \xrightarrow{\quad \beta^- \quad} {}^{87}_{38}\text{Sr}$$

The relative abundances of these isotopes in relation to their own families are 27·2 per cent and 6·96 per cent respectively. Their spins are 3/2 and 9/2. The large spin change $(\varDelta i = \frac{6}{2})$ involved in the transformation is associated with the long half-life of $^{87}_{37}$Rb, which is about 7×10^{10} years. As accurate a measurement as possible of the two unknowns, the half-life of the active rubidium isotope and the proportion of $^{87}_{38}$Sr found in a rubidium bearing mineral, provides an obvious method of estimating the age of the mineral, a topic of great interest.

The other case of a naturally occurring adjacent isobar in which one member is unstable is

$$^{187}_{76}\text{Os} \longrightarrow \ ^{187}_{75}\text{Re}$$

This is a case of K-capture by osmium.

A study of these examples and of what has been said concerning energy changes suggests that the rules governing the occurrence of isobars in nature are accounted for by the criteria of β-decay. If two isobars of adjacent elements have masses which differ by howsoever small an amount in some cases, by an amount greater than $2m_0$ in others, the one with greater mass will be unstable with respect to the other and will disintegrate by β-decay or K-capture to form the nuclide of smaller mass. A familiar example is the decay of tritium :

$$^{3}_{1}\text{H} \ \xrightarrow{\ \beta^- \ } \ ^{3}_{2}\text{He}$$

The mass of $^{3}_{1}\text{H}$ exceeds that of $^{3}_{2}\text{He}$ by about $0·000013$ mu, i.e. $0·012$ MeV. This mass difference is very small, both relatively and absolutely, but it is sufficient.

There are good reasons, therefore, for believing that isobars with atomic numbers differing by unity cannot both be stable. Where cases seem to exist in nature—and the exceptional cases are shown in the ZN diagram (Fig. 5.1)—it is highly probable that the heavier will prove to be radioactive. There are, of course, many examples of *artificial* adjacent isobars in which one or all the members of the group are radioactive.

The stability of isobaric pairs and triplets having atomic numbers which differ by two units is readily accounted for. Consider as an example the isobaric pair :

$$^{50}_{22}\text{Ti} \quad [^{50}_{23}\text{V}] \quad ^{50}_{24}\text{Cr}$$

If we may suppose that the mass of $^{50}_{22}\text{Ti}$ is greater than that of $^{50}_{24}\text{Cr}$, then it may be transformed into the latter by *double β-decay*. It cannot undergo this transformation by two successive single β-decay processes because the mass of the intermediate radionuclide $^{50}_{23}\text{V}$ which would be formed is greater than that of $^{50}_{22}\text{Ti}$. In fact, $^{50}_{23}\text{V}$ itself is unstable. Now the probability that two negatrons will be ejected *simultaneously* from the nucleus $^{50}_{22}\text{Ti}$ to form $^{50}_{24}\text{Cr}$ is vanishingly small. Hence

$_{22}^{50}$Ti is stable. On the other hand, if the mass of $_{24}^{50}$Cr exceeds that of $_{22}^{50}$Ti, a similar argument applies. The simultaneous ejection of two positrons by $_{24}^{50}$Cr to form $_{22}^{50}$Ti, while not impossible, would be so rare an event that this element, too, must be regarded as *stable*. As we shall see, it is a rule that, when two isobars are separated by a third isobar of greater mass than either of the other two, these two are stable.

An interesting class of isobars is the *mirror nuclides* to which reference was made in Chap. II. If two nuclides are such that one is changed into the other by changing either a proton into a neutron or a neutron into a proton, they are called mirror nuclides. For example, $_7^{15}$N and $_8^{15}$O are mirror nuclides. Knowledge of the binding energies of such a pair affords a means of estimating the radius of the nucleus. In all such pairs one member is unstable against beta decay.

From Table 4.2 we see that, of a total of 166 nuclides having even mass numbers, 162 have an even number of protons associated with an even number of neutrons. This preponderance may now be explained by making a simple assumption. We suppose that nuclides of even A have lower energy, that is, smaller mass, when Z is even than when Z is odd. Then, the atomic mass of a nuclide with even A and odd Z being greater than that of either of its isobaric neighbours it can decay into one or the other by electron emission or K-capture. Both neighbours may be stable so that there will occur an instance of a pair of stable isobars of even mass number with atomic numbers differing by two units. It has been noted that for A even there are more than 50 cases of such isobaric pairs.

Relative Stability of Isobars

It is convenient at this point to discuss a matter of considerable interest—the relative stability of members of an isobaric series. It may be considered in relation to the ZN diagram which forms the background of much that is discussed in these pages. A three-dimensional ZN representation of the nuclides showing binding energies (negative quantities) set out along the axis which is normal to the ZN plane would reveal a line of minimum energies which has been called *the valley of stability*. The section of this valley by the plane $Z + N = constant$ would

be a curve shaped approximately like a parabola (Fig. 8.2C).
This curve is the locus of isobars. By studying these curves
we can find a qualitative explanation of the observation that
no stable isobars of odd mass number exist whereas there are
many stable isobars of even mass number. The quantitative
basis of the relation between binding energies and mass numbers
is discussed in the next Chapter. It will there be shown that
the net binding energy of a nucleus may be analysed into a
number of components. For the present we consider four :
(i) the binding energy which is a function of the total number
of nucleons present ; (ii) the component which depends on
saturated nuclear forces ; (iii) the Coulomb energy ; and
(iv) what is called " the odd-even effect ".

In a series of isobars the total number of nucleons is the same
for each member of the series so that the first of these four
factors produces no difference in the binding energy of members
of a group of isobars. The second, however, is not constant.
The main contribution to the binding energy of a nucleus is that
due to the saturated forces between pairs of nucleons—proton-
proton, proton-neutron and neutron-neutron. There is reason
to think, moreover, that the p-p and n-n forces affecting
nucleons in the same state are about equal and that neither is as
great as the p-n force.

With this in mind consider a nuclide having a large neutron
excess ; it would be found high up on the north-western slopes
of the valley of stability. If by negatron emission a neutron is
changed into a proton, a decrease of the n-n forces and an
increase of the p-n forces will occur so that there is, in respect
of these two attractive forces, a net increase of (negative)
binding energy with increasing atomic number. This is
represented in curve A, Fig. 8.2.

The third contribution to the binding energy comes from the
mutual repulsion of the protons. As Z increases, that is, as a
proton replaces a neutron in passing from one to the next
member of the isobaric series, the electrostatic energy will
reduce the total binding energy. This is represented by curve
B, Fig. 8.2. The result of adding the ordinates of curves A and
B is some such parabola-like curve as C, which shows how the
total binding energy varies with Z.

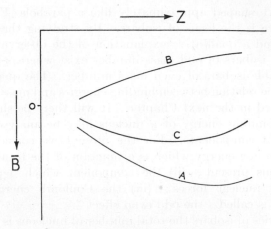

FIG. 8.2. Binding energy of isobars.

Lastly, the odd-even character of the nucleus must be taken
into account. Nuclides with even mass number are of two
types : (i) those in which Z is even and N is even—the *even-even*
type, and (ii) those in which both Z and N are odd—the *odd-odd*
type. Nuclides with odd mass number are also of two types :
(iii) those in which Z is even and N is odd—the *even-odd* type,
and (iv) those in which Z is odd and N is even—the *odd-even*
type.

The successive members of an isobaric series of even mass
number, which must therefore alternate between even-even and
odd-odd types, alternate also in stability to a marked degree.
The series usually contains one or more nuclides which are
stable : these are the even-even type. The intervening odd-
odd nuclides are without exception unstable for A greater than
14. On the other hand, the stability of the members of an
isobaric series of odd mass number is unaffected by the even-
odd, odd-even alternation ; whether the nucleus contains an
odd proton or an odd neutron makes but little difference to the
binding energy.

Consider now in the first instance an isobaric series of odd
mass number. Let us enquire how the binding energy will vary
as the atomic number increases. The net effect of the saturated
nuclear forces and of the electrostatic repulsion is shown in Fig.

8.2 (C). The odd-even effect is roughly constant. The values of the binding energies in relation to atomic number will therefore be found on a curve shaped somewhat like a parabola

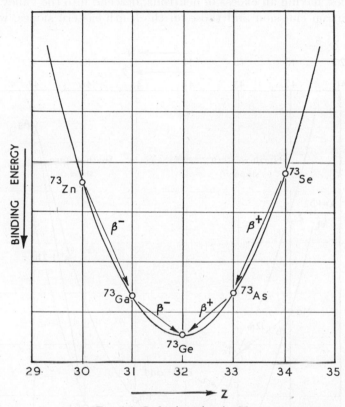

FIG. 8.3. Isobaric series $A = 73$.

having a minimum value. Such a curve is shown in Fig. 8.3. This curve represents the isobaric series $A = 73$. It is a section of the valley of stability made by the plane $Z + N = 73$. The most stable member of the series, the one with the maximum (negative) binding energy is $^{73}_{32}Ge$. It lies at the base of the valley. The probability that two adjacent members of a series of isobars lie at precisely the same level is negligibly small. The nuclide occupying the higher point on the curve will be transformed, even though very slowly, into its neighbour at the lower situation.   This accords with the observation that in an isobaric series of odd mass number there is only one stable nuclide.   It will be clear from Fig. 8.3 that nuclides on the north-western slopes, having an excess of neutrons, descend into the valley by negatron emission and those on the south-eastern slopes, with

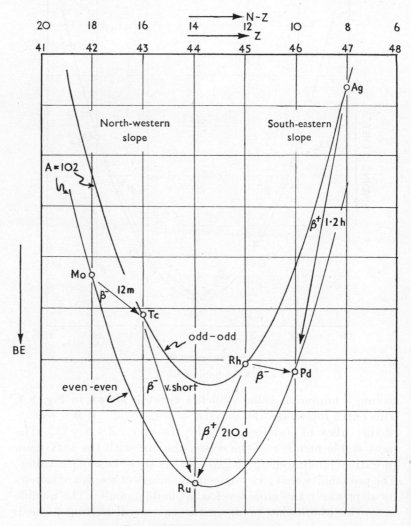

FIG. 8.4. Isobaric series $A = 102$.

a deficiency of neutrons, descend by positron emission or K-capture.

Consider in the second place an isobaric series of even mass number. The odd-even effect now produces a marked contrast in binding energies. The even-even nuclides lie on a parabola-like curve of greater (negative) binding energy. The odd-odd nuclides are found on a curve of similar shape at a higher energy level. This is represented in Fig. 8.4 for mass number 102. It is to be expected that the nuclides on the upper curve will be unstable with respect to those on the lower curve. As a consequence no odd-odd stable nuclei should exist. This is confirmed by observation, with the exception of four nuclides having equal numbers of protons and neutrons : ^2_1H, ^6_3Li, $^{10}_5B$, $^{14}_7N$. The nuclides on the lower curve, the even-even type, are stable except when they are at a higher energy level than some nuclide on the upper curve.

At the lower parts of the lower curve (Fig. 8.4) lie the two stable isotopes $^{102}_{44}Ru$ and $^{102}_{46}Pd$. The nuclide $^{102}_{45}Rh$ lies near the minimum of the upper curve between these two stable nuclides. It is accordingly possible for this odd-odd nuclide to decay by both negatron and positron emission. There are several other nuclides which exhibit the dual mode of decay. They are in every case odd-odd nuclides lying between two stable nuclides. There are other odd-odd nuclides which exhibit either negatron decay (e.g. $^{136}_{55}Cs$, Fig. 8.5) or positron decay ($^{136}_{57}La$), but not both.

It should be noted that the binding energies attributed to the nuclides in Figs. 8.4 and 8.5 are not quantitatively exact. They exhibit in a qualitative way the fact that, if one element is unstable with respect to another, or it may be with respect to two others, the latter lie at a lower energy level.

The useful figure of the valley of stability suggests that the higher a nuclide lies on the valley slopes the greater is its instability as measured by the energy of the emitted β-particle or by the length of the half-life. This is in general true though not invariably so. An example is the isobaric series $A = 85$, which is represented in Fig. 8.6. It will be observed that the half-life increases as stability is approached, whether the access be from the region of neutron excess or from that of neutron deficiency.

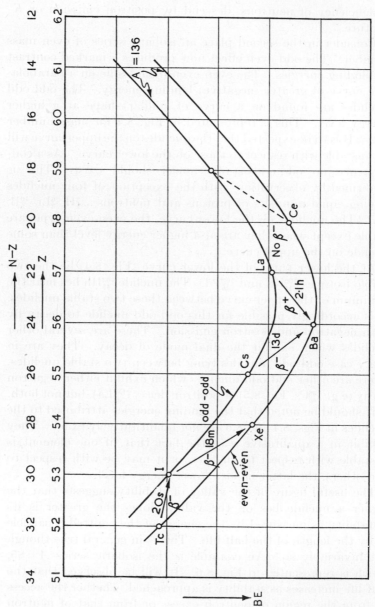

Fig. 8.5. Isobaric series $A = 136$.

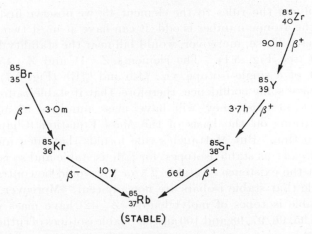

Fig. 8.6. Isobaric series $A = 85$.

A similar effect is observed with isobars of even mass number provided that the odd-odd and even-even are separated into two parallel series.

These considerations suggest that, if an isobaric series is incomplete on account of lack of information in respect of some member of the series, the properties of the missing radionuclide may be roughly predicted in respect of the mode of its decay and the duration of its half-life. For instance, referring again to the isobaric series $A = 85$, if the unknown radionuclide $^{85}_{34}Se$ should at some future time be artificially produced, it is highly probable that it will prove to be a negatron emitter with a half-life of a few seconds or less.

The Missing Elements

Elements of atomic number 43 and 61 are not found in nature. Although claims to have isolated them have been made from time to time these claims have not been substantiated. There is reason to believe, on the basis of rules discussed in this Chapter, that the elements are unstable and therefore, unless their half-lives were of the order of 10^8 years or greater, they would not be found in the earth's crust.

Applying the rules to the element 43, we observe first that, since the atomic number is odd, it can have at most two stable isotopes. These, moreover, would fall near the stability line at $A = 98$ (see Fig. 5.1). The elements $Z = 41$ and $Z = 45$ each consist of a single isotope, viz. $^{93}_{41}\mathrm{Cb}$ and $^{103}_{45}\mathrm{Rh}$ (Fig. 8.7). We may have some confidence, therefore, that if stable isotopes of element 43 exist they will have mass numbers 97 and 99. Calculations on the basis of the Mass Equation (Chap. IX) confirm this. But Mattauch's rule forbids that such nuclides should exist as stable isotopes, for $^{97}_{42}\mathrm{Mo}$ is stable and so is $^{99}_{44}\mathrm{Ru}$, so that the existence of stable $^{97}_{43}\mathrm{X}$ or $^{99}_{43}\mathrm{X}$ would be contrary to the rule that stable isobars are not adjacent. Moreover, since the stable isotopes of molybdenum ($Z = 42$) have mass values 92, 94, 95, 96, 97, 98 and 100 and the stable isotopes of ruthenium ($Z = 44$) have mass values 96, 98, 99, 100, 101, 102 and 104, the mass number of a stable element 43 must, if Mattauch's rule is observed, be as low as 93 or as high as 103, which happen to be the mass values of the single stable isotopes of columbium and rhenium respectively (Fig. 8.7). It appears therefore that the element of atomic number 43 is unlikely to be stable.

These arguments have been justified by the isolation of element 43 by artificial methods. It was prepared in 1937 by C. Perrier and E. Segré who produced it in small amounts by bombarding molybdenum with deuterons. They named it *technetium*. Since then it has been produced in larger quantities as a fission product. Its properties have been studied by the methods of micro-chemistry and it has been assigned to its appropriate place in the chemist's Periodic Table. The $^{99}_{43}\mathrm{Tc}$ isotope has a long half-life of about a million years, while the half-life of $^{97}_{43}\mathrm{Tc}$ is 93 days.

A somewhat similar account may be given of element 61. A calculation based on the Mass Equation shows that the most stable isotopes of this element will have mass numbers 145 and 147 but the existence of the two stable nuclides $^{145}_{60}\mathrm{Nd}$ and $^{147}_{62}\mathrm{Sm}$ makes it improbable (Mattauch's rule) that isotopes of element 61 having mass number 145 and 147 will be stable. The mass numbers of stable isotopes of neodymium being 142, 143, 144, 145, 146, 148 and 150 and those of stable isotopes of samarium being 144, 147, 148, 149, 150, 154, the mass number of a stable

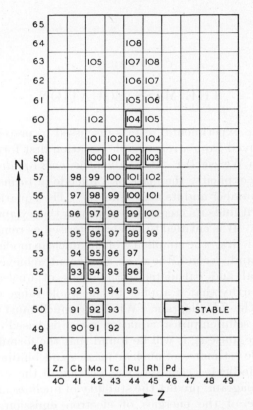

FIG. 8.7. The missing element 43 and its neighbouring isotope families.

isotope of element 61 would have to be as low as 141 or as high as 151. Both of these are too remote from the stability line to be stable.

As in the case of element 43, an isotope of element 61 has been found as a product of fission. Its mass number is 147 and its half-life is 3·7 years. It is a rare earth and it has been named *promethium* by Marinsky and Glendenin who isolated and identified it. The isotope $^{145}_{61}Pr$ has not been found.

REFERENCES

Metzer and Deutsch, 1948, *Phys. Rev.*, **74**, 1640.
Stewart, 1918, *Phil. Mag.*, **36**, 326.

CHAPTER IX

THE MASS EQUATION

MANY of the experimental results discussed in preceding pages may be derived from a remarkable equation first formulated in 1935 by von Weizsäcker. It is called the *mass equation* because it expresses explicitly the mass of a nuclide in terms involving its atomic number and its mass number. The equation is semi-empirical ; it finds its credentials partly in theory and partly in experiment. It is entitled to be characterised as remarkable on two counts : first, the simplicity of the nuclear model on which it is based and, second, the close agreement achieved between experimental and calculated estimations of nuclear masses. It is noteworthy that it applies to the whole range of nuclides plotted on the ZN diagram. While too much must not be expected of a semi-empirical equation which is based on a rough model of the nucleus, it will be found that the formula will not only provide estimates of nuclear masses and binding energies, it will also indicate accurately the location of the stability line in the ZN diagram, predict the stability of nuclides and provide an estimate of the energies of electron emission by radio-nuclides. It has also applications to isobaric series, to the properties of " missing " nuclei and to the phenomenon of fission.

It does not detract from the value of the mass equation that it is based on a crude model which can have but little correspondence with the reality. It is doubtful, perhaps, whether any model, since it must be constructed from concepts of the macrocosmic world, can be related to the " real nucleus ". This is no cause for discouragement. The achievements of the kinetic theory of gases are not less valuable because they are based on a crude atomic model which compares an atom with a perfectly elastic billiard ball. The success of the Bohr planetary electron atom in interpreting spectra is not disqualified on the ground that quantum mechanics disavows any picture of planetary electrons. It may well be that no picture of the nucleus comprehensible by mortal minds can ever be drawn. Nevertheless a rough model may still be a helpful guide to thinking and this is assuredly true of that model of the nucleus which is due to Niels Bohr (1936), to whom also goes much of the credit for the accepted concept of atomic structure.

Liquid Drop Model

Bohr pointed out that the nucleus of the atom behaved as though it had some of the properties of a drop of liquid. The points of similarity may be briefly mentioned.

(1) We have seen that the density of all nuclei is the same, viz., about $2 \cdot 2 \times 10^{14}$ gm. cm.$^{-3}$. Since the density of drops of the same liquid is the same, whatever their diameter may be, this suggests the existence of a " nuclear fluid " which condenses into small drops of different sizes.

(2) The deviation of nuclei from the spherical shape, when it exists, is small, like that of a falling rain-drop subject to slightly anisotropic pressure.

(3) The forces that operate between the molecules of a liquid drop are short-range forces, each molecule being influenced only by its immediate neighbours. The forces between the nucleons of a nucleus—the p-n, p-p and n-n forces—are also short-range forces.

(4) A liquid drop owes its existence to surface tension forces. These determine its shape, its maximum size and its period of vibration when it is slightly distorted from its spherical shape and released. The nucleus also displays surface tension effects due to similar causes, viz., the asymmetry of the forces acting on nucleons situated in the surface of the nucleus.

(5) When heat radiation impinges on a liquid drop, the energy of the photons is shared among the thermally agitated molecules and evaporation occurs : the molecules with the greatest kinetic energy are ejected. In a similar way, when gamma radiation or an energetic particle is incident upon a nucleus it distributes its energy among the constituent nucleons. After a lapse of time, which may be considerable on the nuclear time scale, " evaporation " occurs and a nucleon or a quantum is ejected.

(6) If a liquid drop which is massive relative to the surface tension forces is caused to vibrate, it will break up into drops of smaller size. This is roughly analogous to nuclear fission.

(7) As a liquid drop grows in size the cohesive and disruptive forces which affect it change. A limit is therefore set to the size of a stable drop of liquid. Similarly, there is a limit to the size of a nucleus which finds expression in the termination of the line of stability of the ZN diagram in the region $Z = 82$ to $Z = 92$.

In contrast with these points of resemblance between the properties of the nucleus and those of a drop of liquid, there are certain relevant differences. The nucleons are relatively few in number in comparison with the number of molecules in the smallest drop of liquid. Hence a large proportion lie on the surface. Also, the cohesive forces between nucleons are incomparably greater than those between molecules. Moreover, some of the nucleons carry a positive electric charge giving rise to a disruptive force which has no analogy in a drop of liquid.

Terms of the Equation

The liquid drop model of the nucleus was used by von Weizsäcker to explain nuclear binding energies and as a basis of an equation for estimating their values. The several parts of this equation, which expresses the mass of a nucleus in terms of its mass number A and its atomic number Z, will now be discussed. The equation comprises eight terms. These terms and their mode of derivation are given individual consideration in the following pages. They are finally assembled into one expression which, it will be found, provides accurate values of atomic masses and binding energies as functions of atomic number and mass number.

(1) *The Nucleons.* The main contribution to the mass of a nucleus, $_Z^A M$, is the sum of the masses of Z protons and $N (= A - Z)$ neutrons in their free state. If m_p is the mass of a proton and m_n that of a neutron, we have

$$\text{Mass of } A \text{ nucleons} = Z m_p + N m_n \tag{9.1}$$

But the mass of a nucleus differs from this by the mass defect. We must accordingly add to this the negative binding energy of the nucleus expressed in atomic mass units. The binding energy is the sum of a number of components which are considered separately.

(2) *The Volume Energy.* The first and largest term of the binding energy is due to the interaction of the nucleons at very short distances. As we have seen, nuclear forces are short-range forces, each nucleon attracting only its immediate neighbours. In this respect they differ from long-range forces such as gravitational or electrostatic forces.

The nuclear forces are *saturated.* " Saturation " is a phenomenon familiar to chemists : chemical binding is a saturation force. In such compounds as methane (CH_4), for instance, the carbon bonds are filled completely by four hydrogen atoms which are held to the carbon atom by " exchange " forces. Nuclear forces may also be exchange forces. The saturation character of nuclear forces is clear from Fig. 7.3, for if the forces acting on a single nucleon were long-range deriving from the A nucleons in the nucleus the total binding energy would be proportional to $A(A-1)$. But Fig. 7.3 shows that these forces are independent of A over a considerable range of atomic mass values. Thus we may assume that a nucleon interacts only with its immediate neighbours, the forces between them being accordingly saturated. This conclusion is confirmed by nuclear scattering experiments and by the observation that nuclear radii are well defined (Chap. II).

Thus, the mass of the nucleus is less than that of its separated constituent nucleons by a mass a_1A since this mass, or its energy equivalent, must be supplied to the nucleus to achieve a complete separation of the nucleons. The coefficient a_1 is a constant the value of which has to be determined. To a first approximation, therefore, the mass of the nucleus $_Z^A M$ is obtained by adding a negative term, $-a_1A$, to $Zm_p + Nm_n$, as binding energy per nucleon

$$\text{Volume energy} = -a_1A \qquad (9.2)$$

This is shown in curve (i), Fig. 9.1, as binding energy per nucleon.

(3) *Surface Energy.* The deduction to be made in accordance with Eq. (9.2) is an overestimate because it assumes that each nucleon is surrounded by the same number of other nucleons, whereas surface nucleons, like surface molecules in a liquid

L   H.N.S.

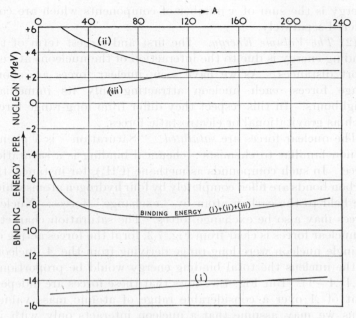

FIG. 9.1. Terms of the Mass Equation.

drop, are not so surrounded and therefore are not as tightly bound as those in the interior. An adjustment must accordingly be made by the addition of a term proportional to the surface area of the nucleus. This is a specially significant correction in the case of light nuclei since the surface energy per unit volume is greater the smaller the nucleus. The volume of nucleus being proportional to A (Chap. II), its surface area is proportional to $A^{\frac{2}{3}}$. Thus the contribution due to surface energy is given by

$$\text{Surface energy} = +a_2 A^{\frac{2}{3}} \qquad (9.3)$$

This is plotted in curve (ii) of Fig. 9.1.

It is of interest to estimate the value of this surface tension for a light nucleus. We shall find later that the value of a_2 is 0·014. Taking $A = 8$, the surface energy is 0·056 mu, i.e., 52 MeV or 83·2 × 10⁻⁶ ergs (Appendix I). Writing γ as the surface tension and r as the radius of the nucleus,

$$4\pi r^2 \,.\, \gamma = 83\cdot2 \times 10^{-6} \text{ ergs} \qquad (9.4)$$

Taking $r = 1 \cdot 5 \times A^{\frac{1}{3}} \cdot 10^{-13} = 3 \times 10^{-13}$ cm. (Chap. II),

$$\gamma \sim 10^{20} \text{ dynes cm.}^{-1}$$

This may be compared with the surface tension of water, 75 dynes cm.$^{-1}$. Thus γ for $A = 8$ is approximately one thousand million tons weight per centimetre!

(4) *Electrostatic Energy.* The mutual repulsion of the protons being a long-range force, each proton affects all the others. This Coulomb energy is disruptive and diminishes the total (negative) binding energy. The number of pairs of protons in a nucleus containing Z protons is $Z(Z-1)/2$ and it may be proved (*v.* Appendix II) that their total Coulomb energy is

$$3e^2 Z(Z-1)/5r,$$

where e is the electronic charge and r is the nuclear radius. Writing Z for $(Z-1)$ and remembering that r is proportional to $A^{\frac{1}{3}}$, we have

$$\text{Electrostatic energy} = + a_3 Z^2 / A^{\frac{1}{3}} \qquad (9.5)$$

This is plotted in curve (iii) of Fig. 9.1. It is clear from this figure that the falling away of the binding energy in the heavy nuclei is largely a consequence of the increase in the electrostatic energy.

The results set out in Eqs. (9.1), (9.2), (9.3) and (9.5) are now brought together in Eq. (9.6).

$$_Z^A M = Zm_p + Nm_n - a_1 A + a_2 A^{\frac{2}{3}} + a_3 Z^2 / A^{\frac{1}{3}} \qquad (9.6)$$

The relative values of the contributions to the mass $_Z^A M$ of the five terms on the right hand side of this equation may be found by considering a definite example. Consider the isotope $_{20}^{40}$Ca. The values of the coefficients a_1, a_2 and a_3 are determined on pp. 148 and 188. The substitution of numerical values in Eq. (9.6) gives

$$_Z^A M = 20(1 \cdot 00813) + 20(1 \cdot 00894) - (0 \cdot 01504)40 + (0 \cdot 014)(40)^{\frac{2}{3}}$$
$$+ 0 \cdot 000627 \frac{(20)^2}{(40)^{\frac{1}{3}}}.$$

This may be set out as under :

		mu
1.	Mass of protons	20·1626
2.	Mass of neutrons	20·1788
3.	Volume energy	− 0·6016
4.	Surface energy	0·1637
5.	Electrostatic energy	0·0734
	Mass of $^{40}_{20}$Ca	39·9769

This calculated result compares with the experimental mass of 39·9754.

The number of protons in $^{40}_{20}$Ca is equal to the number of neutrons, but for all nuclides heavier than this there is an excess of neutrons proportional to $\left(\dfrac{A}{2} - Z\right)$, which increases with Z, and we have seen that this is a factor which affects the binding energy. It may be called the " neutron excess energy ".

(5) *Neutron excess energy.* In considering isobars we found that either an excess or a deficiency of neutrons led to instability. Hence, for nuclides heavier than $^{40}_{20}$Ca, an empirical term involving $\left(\dfrac{A}{2} - Z\right)$, which vanishes for $Z = A/2$, is required. The method of deriving the precise form of this term lies outside the scope of this book. For a discussion reference may be made to a lecture by E. Fermi (1950). It is expressed thus :

$$\text{Neutron excess energy} = + a_4 \frac{\left(\dfrac{A}{2} - Z\right)^2}{A} . \qquad (9.7)$$

Finally, the mass of a nucleus is affected by a component of the binding energy which depends upon whether the numbers of protons and neutrons are even or odd. This factor is a consequence of the pairing of nuclear spins.

(6) *Spin effect energy.* This contribution, while relatively small for heavy nuclides, is not negligible for light nuclides. The rigorous theory of this effect would be out of place here, but a qualitative explanation of the influence of this factor is possible. There are four cases :

(i) *Even-even* nuclei are exceptionally stable. This is attributable to the pairing of all nuclear spins, producing an addition to the binding energy which may be written $-\delta$. This is a function of A and is equal to $a_5/A^{\frac{3}{4}}$.

(ii) *Odd-odd* nuclei are unstable. The contribution to the binding energy in respect of these is $+\delta$, corresponding to the presence of both a proton and a neutron with unpaired spins.

(iii) *Odd-even* and *even-odd* nuclei are of intermediate stability and the contribution δ is taken to be zero.

Summarising, we have

$$\text{Spin effect energy} = \delta \qquad (9.8)$$

where $\delta = \pm a_5/A^{\frac{3}{4}}$ for odd-odd and even-even nuclei respectively and $\delta = 0$ for both even-odd and odd-even nuclei.

It is now possible to assemble all the terms of the mass equation as follows :

$$\,_Z^A M = Zm_p + Nm_n - a_1 A + a_2 A^{\frac{2}{3}} + a_3 \frac{Z^2}{A^{\frac{1}{3}}} + a_4 \frac{\left(\frac{A}{2} - Z\right)^2}{A} + \delta \qquad (9.9)$$

If the binding energy of a nucleus is required we have

$$BE = a_1 A - a_2 A^{\frac{2}{3}} - a_3 \frac{Z^2}{A^{\frac{1}{3}}} - a_4 \frac{\left(\frac{A}{2} - Z\right)^2}{A} - \delta \qquad (9.10)$$

Values of Coefficients

Before applying these equations to the calculation of nuclear mass or energy, we must determine the values of the five coefficients a.

The value of a_3 may be obtained immediately from electrical theory. It is shown in Appendix II to be 0·000627.

The value of a_4 is derived as follows. Consider an isobaric series. As Z varies, while A remains constant, $\,_Z^A M$ varies and passes through a minimum value corresponding to the most stable element of the series. The value of Z corresponding to the minimum mass, Z_0, is found by differentiating Eq. (9.9) with respect to Z and equating the result to zero. Remembering that $N = A - Z$, we have

$$\left(\frac{\partial M}{\partial Z}\right)_A = m_p - m_n + 2a_3 \frac{Z_0}{A^{\frac{1}{3}}} - a_4 \frac{A - 2Z_0}{A} = 0 \qquad (9.11)$$

Thus

$$Z_0 = \frac{m_n - m_p + a_4}{2(a_3 A^{-\frac{1}{3}} + a_4 A^{-1})}$$

Substituting numerical values for the constants,

$$Z_0 = \frac{84 + 10^5 a_4}{62 \cdot 7 A^{\frac{2}{3}} + 10^5 a_4} \cdot \frac{A}{2} \tag{9.12}$$

From this equation the values of a_4 for various stable elements may be calculated. Considering medium-weight elements, $a_4 = 0 \cdot 072$, whence Eq. (9.12) becomes

$$Z_0 = \frac{A}{0 \cdot 017 A^{2/3} + 1 \cdot 98} \tag{9.13}$$

For heavy elements

$$Z_0 = \frac{A}{0 \cdot 084 A^{2/3} + 1 \cdot 98} \tag{9.14}$$

For light elements

$$Z_0 = \frac{A}{0 \cdot 124 A^{2/3} + 1 \cdot 98} \tag{9.15}$$

Since $A = N + Z_0$, for the most stable nuclide we have approximately

$$N/Z_0 = 1 + 0 \cdot 072 A^{\frac{2}{3}} \tag{9.16}$$

From this it is clear that for light nuclides the neutron-proton ratio is unity and that the ratio increases with $A^{\frac{2}{3}}$.

Eqs. (9.13), (9.14) and (9.15) predict the values of Z for the most stable nuclides for the whole ZN diagram, that is from $Z = 0$ to $Z = 92$ so that these three equations show the whole course of the valley of stability.

The values of a_3 and a_4 may now be inserted in Eq. (9.9) and, taking even-odd and odd-even elements for which $\delta = 0$, an equation is obtained which involves a_1 and a_2. The values of these coefficients may now be calculated, for we have a large number of pairs of simultaneous equations, the problem being over-determined. Calculation shows that

$$a_1 = 0 \cdot 01504 \text{ and } a_2 = 0 \cdot 014$$

Using atomic mass units and writing $A - Z$ for N, Eq. (9.9) in its final form is therefore

$$\begin{aligned}
{}^{A}_{Z}M = 0{\cdot}99387A - 0{\cdot}00081Z + 0{\cdot}014A^{\frac{2}{3}} + 0{\cdot}000627\frac{Z}{A^{1/3}} \\
+ 0{\cdot}072\frac{\left(\dfrac{A}{2} - Z\right)^{2}}{A} + \delta \quad (9.17)
\end{aligned}$$

TABLE 9.1

TEST OF SEMI-EMPIRICAL MASS FORMULA

Nucleus	Mass from Formula (mu)	Experimental Mass(mu)
${}^{16}_{8}$O	15·99615	16·00000
${}^{52}_{24}$Cr	51·959	51·956
${}^{98}_{42}$Mo	97·946	97·943
${}^{197}_{79}$Au	197·04	197·04
${}^{238}_{92}$U	238·12	238·12

This mass equation is, as we have said, a remarkable equation in two respects : first, in the simplicity of the theory underlying it and second, in the accuracy of its prediction of nuclear mass This is shown for a few examples in Table 9.1.

The accuracy of the formula (9.9) has been improved in detail by various investigators. In particular Metropolis (1948) has applied a refined formula with considerable increase of accuracy :

$$ {}^{A}_{Z}M = 1014{\cdot}64A + 14A^{\frac{2}{3}} + 41{\cdot}905\,(Z - Z_A)^2/Z_A - 41{\cdot}905Z_A + \delta $$
$$(9.18\text{A})$$

where
$$ Z_A = 66{\cdot}7A/(A^{\frac{2}{3}} + 132) \qquad (9.18\text{B}) $$

No fewer than five thousand pairs of Z, A values were calculated for isotope masses ranging from ${}^{5}_{3}$M to ${}^{249}_{97}$M, the deviation from experimental values throughout the whole range being remarkably small. Eq. (9.18) is undoubtedly a considerable improvement on Eq. (9.17).

An interesting application of the mass equation is to the calculation of the binding energy of the last neutron in a nucleus. Writing this as $(BE)_n$, we have from Eq. (9.9)

$$(BE)_n = m_n - {}_Z^A M + {}^{A-1}_Z M \qquad (9.19)$$

This is found to be a positive quantity for all stable elements. There is therefore no tendency for these elements to emit neutrons spontaneously. On the other hand, a similar calculation of BE in respect of α-particles shows that (BE) is not always positive. In fact, the value of the expression

$$(BE)_\alpha = m_\alpha - {}_Z^A M + {}^{A-4}_{Z-2} M \qquad (9.20)$$

is negative for medium and higher values of Z. The possible inference is that these nuclides are unstable against α-decay with activities too small to be detected. In the region beyond $Z = 90$ the negative value of $(BE)_\alpha$ increases and α-activity is sufficient to terminate the periodic table.

REFERENCES

N. Bohr, 1936, *Nature*, **137**, 344.

E. Fermi, 1950, *Nuclear Physics*, p. 22.

N. Metropolis, 1948, *Table of Atomic Masses*, Institute for Nuclear Studies, Chicago.

CHAPTER X

NUCLEAR ENERGY LEVELS

THE application of quantum rules to the electron configuration of the atom was so successful in interpreting optical spectra and in providing a rational basis for the periodic classification of the elements that it was natural to look for evidence of quantized energy levels in the nucleus of the atom. It soon became clear that such evidence exists. The nucleus, although it has no central force field as the atom has, can exist nevertheless in one of a series of characteristic discrete energy levels. The law of force for nuclei is not known; the Schrödinger equation as applied to atomic systems is thus not generally applicable to the nucleus. Knowledge of nuclear energy levels has been advanced experimentally by the study of radioactive decay, of resonance phenomena in nuclear reactions and of isomeric transitions.

In general, an excited nuclear energy state is shortlived. It may be caused by the absorption by the nucleus of a quantum of γ-radiation or by the acquisition of an electron, neutron or other particle. Moreover, the emission of a particle by a radioactive nucleus may leave the daughter nucleus in an excited state. After a lifetime of a small fraction of a microsecond the excited nucleus normally makes a transition to a stable state by radiation.

The nuclear energy levels have a finite width. This uncertainty concerning the precise value of the energy of a nuclear state is related to the life-time of the nucleus in that state by the Uncertainty Principle,

$$\Delta t \,.\, \Delta E = \hbar \qquad (10.1)$$

The more precisely the time of a nuclear process is defined, or the shorter the lifetime Δt of the state, the less exact is our knowledge of the energy change. The width of energy levels, that is, the value of ΔE in Eq. (10.1) may vary between 0·1 and 10^5 ev, whence it follows that the duration of the corresponding states lies between 10^{-14} and 10^{-20} seconds.

Ellis (1922) showed in 1922 that the frequencies of the γ-rays of RaB were characterized by additive relations of a simple type : $\nu_1 + \nu_2 = \nu_3$. The analogy of atomic energy levels suggested that the γ-rays were associated with transitions between quantized energy levels in the nucleus.

The existence of energy levels was confirmed by Rutherford's study of the alpha emission of ThC'. He showed that the great majority of α-particles emitted by ThC' had a range in air at normal atmospheric pressure of 8·6 cm. This takes no account of the " straggling " effect due to statistical fluctuations of energy consequent upon random collisions with gaseous molecules. For every million α-particles with this range, there were found 35 particles with a range of 9·7 cm. and 190 with a range of 11·6 cm. (Table 10.1). These " long-range " particles point unequivocally to the existence of energy levels in the ThC'

TABLE 10.1

ThC' : LONG-RANGE ALPHA PARTICLES

Level	Relative Number	Energy (MeV)
0	10^6	8·95
1	35	9·67
2	190	10·75

nucleus. This is illustrated in Fig. 10.1. ThC' is the daughter, by β emission, of ThC. Its half-life in the ground state (level 0) is only 0·3 microseconds and in an excited state even shorter. The most probable process brings the ThC' nucleus to level 0, but occasionally it leaves it in either level 1 or level 2.

From these levels there may be transitions to level 0 with the emission of a γ-ray. However, the life-time of the excited ThC' nucleus is so brief that the emission of an α-particle may precede and thus forestall that of the γ-ray, in which case the α-particle would have an excess of energy equal to that of the γ-ray. Thus, measurement of the energies of long-range α-particles, permit the assignment of energy levels to the *parent* nucleus, ThC'. RaC' also emits long-range particles and twelve energy levels have been measured.

We consider next the case where energy measurements reveal levels in the *daughter* nucleus.

Until 1930 it was believed that, apart from long-range particles, all α-particles emitted by a given radioactive element had the same energy. In this year however, Rosenblum (1930) using a magnetic spectrometer equipped with a magnet weighing over 100 tons and producing a field of 36,000 oersted, showed that the energies of the α-particles of some, but not all, α-emitters were not precisely equal. The α-particles could be divided into groups having almost identical but definitely distinct energies. Rosenblum found this to be the case for the decay of ThC to ThC''. The energies of the groups showing the *fine-structure* of the ThC alpha spectrum are given in Table 10.2. From the Table it is clear that only 27·2% of the α-particles emitted by ThC have

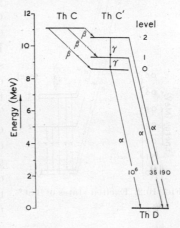

FIG. 10.1. Long-range α-particles from Th C'.

TABLE 10.2

Th C : FINE STRUCTURE OF ALPHA SPECTRUM

Level	Relative Intensity (%)	Energy (MeV)
0	27·2	6·201
1	69·8	6·161
2	1·89	5·873
3	0·16	5·729
4	1·00	5·709

the maximum energy of 6·201 MeV. The energy deficiency of the remaining 72·8% of the particles is stored in the daughter nucleus, ThC'', which may accordingly exist in any one of four excited states of different energies. This is represented in Fig. 10.2.

The excited states are short-lived. The nucleus assumes the ground state, the excess of energy being carried away by the emitted γ-ray. The energies of the γ-ray coincide with measured energy differences in the α-particle groups. It is clear from Fig. 10.2 that some transitions are *forbidden* ; energies associated with other transitions are summarized in Table 10.3. This Table shows the close correlation between the energy differences of α-particles groups and the differences between energy levels of the daughter nucleus as determined by measurement of γ-ray energies.

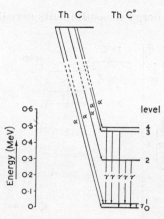

Fig. 10.2. Excited states of ThC″.

TABLE 10.3

ThC″: Gamma Ray Energies

Transitions	Energy difference of α-particle groups	Energy of γ-ray
$l_1 - l_0$	0·040	0·040
$l_2 - l_0$	0·328	0·327
$l_3 - l_0$	0·472	0·471
$l_2 - l_1$	0·288	0·287
$l_3 - l_1$	0·432	0·432
$l_4 - l_1$	0·452	0·451

Evidence of nuclear levels may be found in many of the naturally radioactive elements. The improvement in the accuracy of the measurements with increasing technical resources has confirmed the correspondence between γ-ray energies and the differences in α-particle energies found in the fine structure. Further examples may be found in the classic literature of radioactivity (e.g. Rutherford, Chadwick and Ellis, 1951). In more recent times, knowledge of the energy levels of nuclides has been greatly extended by the study of induced radioactivity.

Term Diagrams

The term diagrams of nuclei are figures of great complexity. The information they summarize is the harvest of a very large number of experiments now undertaken in nuclear physics laboratories all over the world. A relatively simple example of an energy level diagram is that of the radio isotope $_3^8$Li shown in Fig. 10.3. It will be instructive to interpret this

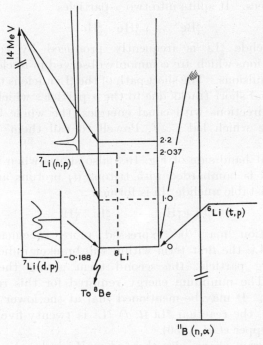

FIG. 10.3. Energy levels of ^{8}Li.

figure since it shows how the results of a large number of experiments are conveniently summarized. It should be remembered that energy level schemes similar to that of Fig. 10.3 are being slowly built up for several hundred nuclides and that the complexity of most of them is not only much greater than that shown here but is increasing rapidly with the accumulation of the results of unceasing investigation.

The inner vertical lines of Fig. 10.3 suggest the potential

energy well of the ^{8}Li nucleus, the line marked 0 being the ground state. The arrow at the base of the diagram indicates that $^8_3$Li is unstable. It decays with the emission of a negatron to one of several energy levels of $^8_4$Be :

$$^8_3\text{Li} \longrightarrow {^8_4\text{Be}} + \beta^-$$

The half-life is 0·825 seconds (Rall and McNeil, 1951). The nucleus $^8_4$Be is itself unstable, having a half-life of about 5×10^{-14} secs. It splits into two α-particles :

$$^8_4\text{Be} \longrightarrow {^4_2\text{He}} + {^4_2\text{He}}$$

The nuclide $^8_3$Li is frequently produced by cosmic ray disintegrations which are commonly observed in nuclear photographic emulsions. The short path of the $^8_3$Li nucleus terminates in two equal short tracks due to the α-particles which move in opposite directions with equal energies, the whole having an appearance which led C. F. Powell to call them " hammer tracks ".

The right hand side of Fig. 10.3 also shows when the stable nuclide $^6_3$Li is bombarded with tritons (t) protons are ejected and the unstable nuclide $^8_3$Li is formed :

$$^6_3\text{Li} + {^3_1\text{H}} \longrightarrow {^8_3\text{Li}} + {^1_1\text{H}}$$

This reaction may be expressed more succinctly thus : ^{6}Li (t, p) ^{8}Li, the first term within the bracket indicating the bombarding particle, the second term giving the emitted particle. The minimum energy required for this reaction is 0·800 MeV. It may be mentioned that at the lower energy of 0·240 MeV. the reaction ^{6}Li (t, d) ^{7}Li is twenty-five times as intense (Pepper *et al.* 1950).

The diagram shows also that when $^7_3$Li is bombarded with neutrons, an excited state of $^8_3$Li may be produced which reverts to the ground state by the emission of γ-radiation : ^{7}Li (n, γ) ^{8}Li. The graph indicates that at an energy slightly higher than the threshold energy the capture cross-section is anomalously high : $\sigma = 33 \pm 5$ mb.

Finally, the interactions of deuterons of energy of about 14 MeV. with $^7_3$Li produces protons : ^{7}Li (d, p) ^{8}Li. These protons are found in two energy groups corresponding to two energy levels in the ^{8}Li nucleus at 1·0 and 2·2 MeV. (Gore and

Harvey, 1951). This is one method by which the energy levels of radioactive nuclei may be determined.

This short account of the term diagrams is sufficient to show that a knowledge of the energy levels of nuclides together with the selection rules of transitions is a useful preliminary to an understanding of nuclear structure. Each nuclide will be characterized by a term diagram of the kind shown in Fig. 10.3. It may be that general rules comprising the energy levels of all nuclides will be discovered, leading to a great co-ordinating principle covering the energy level schemes.

We turn now to a consideration of nuclides in the ground state. For the last twenty years attempts have been made to assign a shell structure to the nucleus as was done for the orbital electrons of the atoms. A considerable impetus to this work has recently come from the discovery of the so-called *magic numbers*. In presenting a short account of this it is assumed that the main points of the theory of atomic structure is familiar to the reader. So brief a digression as the following, outlining the salient features of this topic, cannot do more than bring the relevant points to mind for students who are already familiar with the subject.

Atomic Structure

Bohr's theory of " stationary states " of the atom was put forward to account for the facts of atomic spectra. Bohr started from the surprising postulate, which was in direct contradiction to electromagnetic theory, that an electron moving round a nucleus in a closed orbit did not radiate ; on the contrary, this was called a *stationary state* of the atom. It was only when an atom changes from one stationary state corresponding to an energy E_1 to another such state with energy $E_2 (E_1 > E_2)$ that radiation of frequency v was emitted and the relation held—

$$E_1 - E_2 = hv \qquad (10.2)$$

where h is Planck's constant.

The simplest model of the Bohr atom assumed that the angular momentum of the orbital electron was *quantized* : $mv.r = n$, where n is an integer called the *principal quantum number*. The insertion of energies obtained in this way in Eq. (10.2) produced a significantly close agreement with the measured frequencies of lines of the hydrogen spectrum. A refinement of Bohr's theory, made by Sommerfeld, introduced a second quantum number l, called the *azimuthal quantum number*, with which was associated in the early elementary theory the eccentricity of the elliptical orbits of the electron. The possible values of l, were 0, 1, 2 ... $(n-1)$. Later, a third quantum number, m, called the *magnetic quantum number* with integral values varying from l to $-l$ was introduced to explain the changes in spectra produced by a magnetic field. Finally, a *spin quantum number* s was postulated to account for the grouping of lines in spectra. The spin quantum number can assume two values only : $s = \pm \frac{1}{2}$.

The four quantum numbers are used to define the energy states of the atom. In 1925 Pauli enunciated what is known as the *Exclusion Principle* : *no two electrons in the same atom can have their four quantum numbers n, l, m, s identical*. This simple principle leads directly to the notion that the orbital electrons can be arranged in " shells " and to an explanation of the salient features of the periodic classification of the elements. Consider the case $n = 1$. Corresponding to this there can be only 2 electrons since, as stated above, the possible values of l and m are limited, and $s = \pm \frac{1}{2}$ (Table 10.4).

TABLE 10.4

n	1	1
l	0	0
m	0	0
s	$+\frac{1}{2}$	$-\frac{1}{2}$

If the principal quantum number is $n = 2$, there are 8 possible electron states as set out in Table 10.5.

TABLE 10.5

n	2	2	2	2	2	2	2	2
l	1	1	1	1	1	1	0	0
m	$+1$	$+1$	0	0	-1	-1	0	0
s	$+\frac{1}{2}$	$-\frac{1}{2}$	$+\frac{1}{2}$	$-\frac{1}{2}$	$+\frac{1}{2}$	$-\frac{1}{2}$	$+\frac{1}{2}$	$-\frac{1}{2}$

It is easily shown that the Exclusion Principle requires that the maximum number of electrons in any group is $2n^2$ and that the orbital electrons are arranged in *quantum groups* or *shells* as shown in Table 10.6. The application of this to the periodic classification of the elements will be clear to students with an elementary knowledge of chemistry.

TABLE 10.6

NUMBER OF ELECTRONS IN SUCCESSIVE SHELLS

$l =$	0	1	2	3	4	Total $(2n^2)$
$n = 1$	2					2
2	2	6				8
3	2	6	10			18
4	2	6	10	14		32
5	2	6	10	14	18	50

We conclude this digression with a reference to the method used in spectroscopy of designating a particular electron in an atom. For a full account the reader is referred to works on Atomic Physics (e.g. Tolansky, 1949).

Atoms with *closed* shells are those of the inert elements, helium, neon, etc. Atoms having a closed shell plus a single outer electron are those of the alkali metals, lithium, sodium, etc. This electron can occupy different orbits corresponding to different values of the azimuthal quantum number, l, the orbits being designated by small (lower case) letters which originated earlier in the classification of spectral series (Table 10.7).

TABLE 10.7

Azimuthal quantum number (l)	0 1 2 3 4 5 6 ...
Electron orbit	s p d f g h i ...

The principal quantum number is placed before the small letter so that, for example, an electron designated by $n = 3$ and $l = 1$ is called a $3p$ electron. This shorthand notation is carried

M   H.N.S.

over to the nucleus and is used to characterize the energy levels of nucleons.

The Magic Numbers

The success of atom building in explaining spectra, the periodic table and diverse experimental facts led to attempts at nucleus building and the assignment of shell structures to nuclei. An impetus has been given to these efforts by the discovery that nuclei which contains protons or neutrons of the numbers shown in Table 10.8 are characterized by certain properties which include special stability and superior natural abundance.

TABLE 10.8

MAGIC NUMBERS

Protons	2		8		20		50		82		
Neutrons	2		8		20		50		82		126
Differences		6		12		30		32		44	
Shell	I	II		III		IV		V		VI	

The unusual stability of such groups brings to mind the closed electron shells of the atoms of the inert gases. The differences in Table 10.8 should give the numbers in closed shell configurations. The evidence for the special character of these proton and neutron numbers has been marshalled by Maria G. Mayer (1948). Some items of the evidence which she adduces are set out in summary style in the following paragraphs.

(1) *Absorption cross sections*. The neutron absorption cross section of yttrium with 50 neutrons is the smallest known. The cross sections of lanthanum and praseodymium (82 neutrons) are 7 times and 3 times smaller than that of their neighbours and that of barium (82 neutrons) is 0·03 of that of lanthanum. Exceptionally low cross sections are shown by barium (82 neutrons) bismuth (126 neutrons) and lead (82 protons, 126 neutrons).

(2) *Absolute abundance*. This is obviously closely related to the stability of nuclides. A plot of natural abundance of nuclides against (*a*) number of protons, (*b*) number of neutrons shows peaks corresponding to the following elements :

Zirconium	(50 neutrons)
Tin	(50 protons)
Barium	(82 neutrons)
Tungsten	(82 neutrons)
Lead	(82 protons, 126 neutrons).

(3) *Isotope spread.* By this is meant the difference in mass number between the lightest and heaviest isotopes of a given element. It is a feature of the ZN diagram (Fig. 4.1) and is related to the stability of the nuclides. For calcium, with 20 protons, this difference is 8 neutrons, which is twice as great as that of any of its neighbours in the ZN diagram, tin (50 protons) has 10 isotopes, the largest number of isotopes of any element and the spread is 12. This is equalled in only one other case, that of xenon (82 neutrons). One element has a spread of 10 neutrons, viz. samarium (82 neutrons).

(4) *Isotone spread.* The average number of isotones when N is odd is less than one ; when N is even it is between three and four. The greatest number of isotones for a given N, attained only once in the ZN diagram, is seven, and this is for $N = 82$. Six isotones occur once only, for $N = 50$.

(5) *Isotopic abundance.* As a general rule, for nuclei with $Z > 40$, the abundance of the most abundant isotope of an element does not exceed 35 per cent. There are three exceptions, viz.,

Strontium	$(N = 50)$	82%
Barium	$(N = 82)$	72%
Cerium	$(N = 82)$	90%

Again, for $Z > 42$, the relative abundance of the lightest (neutron-poor) isotopes is less than 2 per cent. There are only five exceptions to this rule, viz. :

Zirconium	$(N = 50)$	48%
Molybdenum	$(N = 50)$	16%
Ruthenium	$(N = 52)$	5%
Neodymium	$(N = 82)$	26%
Samarium	$(N = 82)$	3%

(6) *Delayed neutron emitters.* The nuclides $^{87}_{36}\mathrm{Kr}$ and $^{137}_{54}\mathrm{Xe}$ have 51 and 83 neutrons respectively and the smallest charge

compatible with 50 or 82 neutrons. If these latter neutron groups form closed shells, it may be expected that the binding energies of the 51st and 83rd neutrons will be low. This is borne out by the fact that $^{87}_{36}$Kr and $^{137}_{54}$Xe are the only two delayed neutron emitters known.

The foregoing evidence in support of the view that nuclei are constituted of shells of protons and neutrons—closed shells, corresponding to the magic numbers, having a special degree of stability—is supplemented by recent accurate measurements of the binding energies of nuclides (Duckworth, 1952). A plot of the binding energy per nucleon against mass number for stable nuclides ($Z > 21$) is reproduced in Fig. 10.4. It is to be

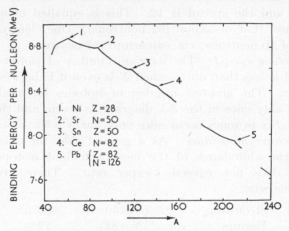

1. Ni $Z = 28$
2. Sr $N = 50$
3. Sn $Z = 50$
4. Ce $N = 82$
5. Pb $\begin{cases} Z = 82 \\ N = 126 \end{cases}$

FIG. 10.4. Stability of magic number nuclei.

expected that, if the completion of a nuclear shell results in a special degree of stability, there should be a sudden change in the gradient of this curve. The figure shows that these changes occur for the cases of nuclides containing 50 and 82 protons and 50, 82 and 126 neutrons. Other kinks occur which may indicate the closing of sub-shells.

One further group of facts is relevant to this discussion. In Chap. XI is given an account of the nuclear species known as *isomers*. Related to this is a phenomenon which has been called "islands of isomerism". It is found that long-lived isomers, with half-lives exceeding 1 second, are correlated with the magic numbers. In Fig. 10.5, which is due to Goldhaber and Hill (1952), are plotted all the isomers of long-life and odd

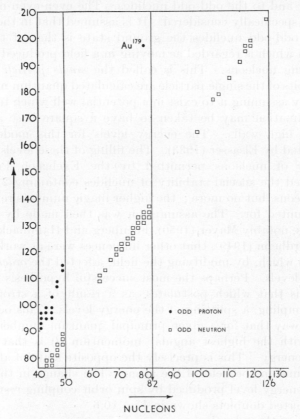

FIG. 10.5. Islands of isomerism : isomers of odd A.

mass number against their odd proton or odd neutron numbers. The grouping of isomers in " islands " below the numbers 50, 82 and 126 is clear.

Shell Structure

This array of evidence for shells in atomic nuclei is impressive and many attempts have been made to correlate hypothetical nuclear energy levels with the numbers of protons and neutrons found in configurations of special stability in a manner closely analogous to that of the orbital electrons. The most successful of these attempts to date has applied to nuclides of odd mass number and to the odd-odd nuclides. The even-even nuclides are not specifically considered. It is assumed that in these odd A and odd-odd nuclides the ground state is that of the odd nucleon which is regarded as moving in a field produced by the remaining nucleons. This is called the *single particle model*. The orbits of the single particle are calculated quantum mechanically by assuming it to exist in a potential well which to a first approximation may be taken to have a square base and infinitely high walls. The energy levels for this model were calculated by Elsasser (1933). The filling of these levels by the number of nucleons permitted by the Exclusion Principle explained the special stability of nuclides containing 2, 8 and 20 nucleons, but no more ; the higher magic numbers remained unaccounted for. The assumption was then made by several workers, notably Mayer (1950), Feenberg and Hammack (1949) and Nordheim (1949), that other influences were at work in the nucleus which, by modifying the field, affected the *order* of the energy levels. Perhaps the most successful hypothesis to date (1954) is that which postulates, as a result of a strong spin orbit coupling, a splitting of the energy levels. This occurs in such a way that for a given principal quantum number n, the state with the highest angular momentum (l) is that of the lowest energy. This is precisely the opposite state of affairs to that found in the field of the atom. The change in the order of the energy level produced by spin orbit coupling resulted in the inverted doublets shown in Fig. 10.6.

Each of these levels can accommodate a maximum number of nucleons in accordance with the Exclusion Principle. These numbers are shown in Fig. 10.6 (last column) and it is clear that the shells obtained in this way correspond exactly with the magic numbers shown in the squares. This success indicates that the single particle model has some value, at least as a first approximation.

The model has further successes to its credit. It leads to a remarkably successful prediction of the known spins of all nuclides of odd mass number from $Z = 1$ to $Z = 83$. This is set forth in Fig. 10.6 as far as $Z = 51$. The energy levels are

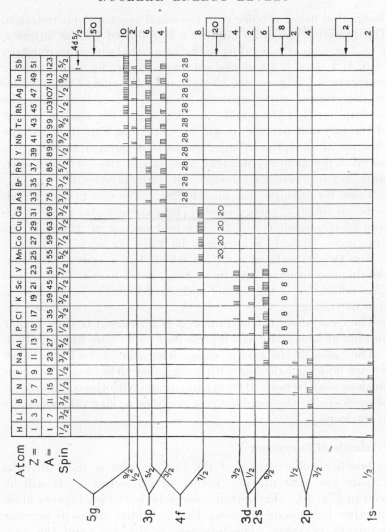

FIG. 10.6. Nuclear shell structure : odd proton nuclei.

designated in accordance with the usual spectroscopic notation. The principal quantum number n is followed by the letters s, p. d, f, g. ... (corresponding to the azimuthal quantum numbers $l = 0$, 1, 2, 3, 4, ...) and the subscript gives the total angular momentum. Figures are also given for the spin of the nuclides as determined experimentally (row 4). Recalling now the assumption that the angular momentum of the nucleus is that of the last odd particle, it will be seen from Fig. 10.6 that the theoretical ascription of spin values is in agreement with that found experimentally in every case except two. Of 64 known spins, 62 are correctly forecast—an impressive result.

Take, for example, the nuclide $^{45}_{21}$Sc. The odd proton is seen to be on the $4f_{7/2}$ energy level. The experimental value of the spin of this nuclide is 7/2. The odd proton of $^{79}_{35}$Br is in the $3p_{3/2}$ level : its spin is known to be 3/2.

The two exceptions are $^{23}_{11}$Na which has a spin of 3/2, and should, according to the hypothesis, have a spin of 5/2, and $^{55}_{25}$Mn which has a spin of 5/2 and should, theoretically, have a spin of 7/2.

The case where the odd nucleon is a neutron is very similar and might be equally well represented by a figure like Fig. 10.6.

The cases of the even-even nuclides cannot be tested since we are no longer dealing with a single particle model, but conclusions may be derived from comparison with the configuration of nucleons in the neighbouring nuclides having odd members of nucleons.

" Islands of Isomerism "

Another achievement of the shell model is its ability to explain the existence of " islands of isomerism ". It will be seen in Fig. 10.6 that certain energy levels which lie very close together correspond to states having widely different angular momenta or spins. One example is the $3p_{1/2}$ and the $5g_{9/2}$ levels. There is a competition between these two levels of almost equal energy for the reception of the next few nucleons after the $4f_{5/2}$ level has been filled. The time of transition from the higher to the lower energy level would be rapid if it were not " highly forbidden " by the change in spin involved. In other words, the spin change affects the probability of the change of energy level and thus the half-life of the isomer is here prolonged. It may have any value from a fraction of a second to several years.

An inspection of Fig. 10.6 leads one to expect therefore that from $Z = 39$ to $Z = 49$, that is, just before the completion of the fourth shell, isomerism should be frequent. In fact, 26 nuclides with odd Z or odd N between these limits 39 to 49 are known to occur in isomeric states. On the other hand, after the level $5g_{9/2}$ has been filled, the competition is between $5g_{7/2}$ and $4d_{5/2}$. We should accordingly not expect to find isomers in the region where these levels are filling. In fact, the first isomer is ^{111}Cd which occurs after both these shells have been completed. Following the completion of the fifth shell (82 nucleons), from 82 to 117, the absence of isomers is again very striking (v. Fig. 10.5, p. 161).

The levels as shown in Fig. 10.6 are drawn as straight lines. In the case, however, of levels as nearly coincident as the $3p_{1/2}$ and $5g_{9/2}$ levels, it would be more correct to show them as *crossing* at certain points so that an isomer such as $^{113}_{49}$In which has a measured spin of 9/2 in the ground state is in the state $p_{1/2}$ when at the higher energy level.

It will be observed that there is incompatibility between the shell model and the liquid drop model of the nucleus. In the former the nucleons are found in states that exist in a potential well and there is little interaction between nucleons in different states. In the latter, the interaction is strong, the mutual repulsion between protons, for example, being considerable. It is now fairly securely established, however, that the hypothesis of shell structure can provide a natural explanation of the distribution of spin values among the nuclides, so far as these are known. The single particle model is an approximation, based on the assumption that the states, spins, parity etc. are due, in the cases of odd A and odd-odd nuclei, to the single odd particle. Crude though it be, the model points unambiguously to the magic numbers, to measured nuclear spins and to the occurrence and locus of the islands of isomerism. The evidence is mostly empirical ; theory lags behind. It is to be anticipated that the accumulation of experimental data relating to nuclear spins and magnetic moments, isomerism and β-decay will lead to the construction of an empirical model of the nucleus which, whether supported by theoretical interpretation or not, will allow a correlation of observations and measurements over a wide range.

REFERENCES

Henry E. Duckworth, 1952, *Nature*, **170**, 158.

Ellis, 1922, *Proc. Roy. Soc.*, A, **101**, 1.

J. Elsasser, 1933, *J. de Phys. et le Rad.*, **4**, 549.

E. Feenberg and K. C. Hammack, 1949, *Phys. Rev.*, **75**, 1877.

M. Goldhaber and R. D. Hill, 1952, *Rev. Mod. Phys.*, **24**, 3, 180.

Gore and Harvey, Jan. 1951, *MIT Prog. Rep.*, p. 46.

M. G. Mayer, 1948, *Phys. Rev.*, **74**, 235.

M. G. Mayer, 1950, *Phys. Rev.*, **78**, 16.

L. W. Nordheim, 1949, *Phys. Rev.*, **75**, 1894.

T. P. Pepper *et al.*, 1952, *Phys. Rev.*, **85**, 155.

W. Rall and K. G. McNeill, 1951, *Phys. Rev.*, **83**, 1244.

S. Rosenblum, 1930, *J. Phys.*, **1**, 438.

E. Rutherford, J. Chadwick and C. D. Ellis, 1951, *Radiations from Radioactive Substances*.

S. Tolansky, (1949), *Introduction to Atomic Physics*.

CHAPTER XI

ISOMERS

THE possibility that two radioactive nuclei might have the same mass and the same charge and yet be distinguishable by some other characteristic such as their disintegration constants was considered by Soddy in 1917. The first case of this kind was established in 1921 when Hahn proved that the natural radioelement $UZ(^{234}_{91}Pa)$ had the same mass and the same charge as the familiar UX_2 but a different rate of decay. No further example was found until induced radioactivity was discovered in 1934. It was then shown that an indium isotope exhibited the same property.

When a nucleus is in an excited state, it usually reverts to the ground state in a time of the order of 10^{-13} seconds or less. In the case of some nuclei, however, the time may be long enough to be measurable, say, 10^{-7} seconds or longer. Such a nucleus is said to be *metastable* and its excited state is distinguished from its ground state by an asterisk : $^A_Z X^*$.

Nuclei of the same mass number and the same atomic number which differ in this way in their state of energy are called *isomers*. The term " isomer " is used also by chemists. Molecules having the same composition but differing in the arrangement of their atoms are called " molecular isomers ". Similarly, nuclear isomers contain the same nucleons differently arranged and in a different state of energy.

The first clearly established case of isomerism among artificially radioactive nuclides was that of bromine (Amaldi *et al.*, 1935). Before we take a general view of isomers as a type of nuclear species, it will be convenient to consider in detail the case of bromine.

It was found that, when bromine was irradiated with thermal neutrons, the product showed three activities characterized by decay rates of 18 min., 4·4 hr. and 34 hr. This was a surprising observation since bromine has only two isotopes, $^{79}_{35}Br$ (50·5%)

and $^{81}_{35}Br$ (49·5%). The possibility that there might be a third isotope was ruled out, for there is no case of a nucleus of odd atomic number greater than unity having more than two isotopes. The two reactions

$$^{79}_{35}Br + n \longrightarrow {}^{80}_{35}Br + \gamma$$
$$^{80}_{35}Br + n \longrightarrow {}^{81}_{35}Br + \gamma$$

give rise to three decay periods, so that either ^{80}Br or ^{81}Br must be an example of isomerism. The half lives were 18·5 min., 4·4 hr. and 34 hr. The identity of the bromine isotope existing in an isomeric state was established by irradiating bromine with γ-rays :

$$^{79}_{35}Br + \gamma \longrightarrow {}^{78}_{35}Br + n$$
$$^{81}_{35}Br + \gamma \longrightarrow {}^{80}_{35}Br + n$$

These two products also had three decay periods, the half lives being 6·4 min., 18·5 min. and 4·4 hr. Thus the 18·5 min. and 4·4 hr. periods are found in both the (n, γ) and the (γ,n) re-

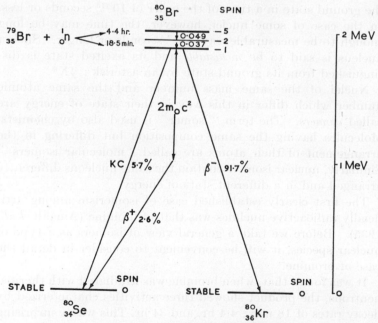

FIG. 11.1. Decay of isomer ^{80}Br.

actions. Since $^{80}_{35}$Br is a product of both reactions, it must be this isotope which exhibits a dual mode of decay.

The isomerism of the ^{80}Br nucleus is explained by supposing that the impact of a neutron on a ^{79}Br nucleus, or of a γ-ray on a ^{81}Br nucleus, produces ^{80}Br nuclei in excited states of high energy. These excited nuclei decay almost immediately by the emission of γ-rays but the product nuclei are found on three metastable energy levels corresponding to three different spin values, viz. 5, 2 and 1. This is shown in Fig. 11.1. The level marked 1 is the ground state.

The conditions of metastability are found here since the change from the higher level to the ground level involves a small energy change and a large change of angular momentum. The level marked 5 is metastable. The process of reversion to the ground state by emission of a γ-ray is called an *isomeric transition*, denoted by the abbreviation I.T.

Immediately after the neutron bombardment of ^{79}Br ceases, the 18·5 min. activity predominates, ^{80}Br nuclei in the ground state decaying in three different ways, all having the same half life period of 18·5 min. :

$$\begin{array}{lll}
 & & \% \\
\nearrow\ ^{80}_{36}Kr + \beta^- & & 91\cdot7 \\
^{80}_{35}Br \rightarrow\ ^{80}_{34}Se\ -\beta^-\ (K\ \text{capture}) & & 5\cdot7 \\
\searrow\ ^{80}_{34}Se\ +\beta^+ & & 2\cdot6
\end{array}$$

After a time, according to a well-known rule of radioactive decay, the predominant activity becomes that of 4·4 hr. period. Nuclei in the metastable state (spin 5) decay to the ground state (spin 1) with the emission of a γ-ray of energy 86 keV. In fact γ-rays of the two energies are observed, viz. 49 and 37 keV. For this reason the intermediate energy level (spin 2) is hypothesized. The half-life of nuclei of this energy will be short since the spin change to that of state 1 is small.

Conclusive confirmation of the facts related above was obtained by the chemical separation of the bromine isomers, the separated products exhibiting the two half-lives. The molecule of a chemical compound of bromine is stable so long as the chemical bond uniting the atoms of the molecule is secure. If however, a γ-ray from ^{80}Br* is " internally converted ", that

is, transfers its energy to an electron which is ejected, the
" conversion electron " may destroy the chemical bond, thereby
liberating the bromine ion to form another chemical compound
which is chemically separable from the first. The process is
somewhat similar to the Szilard-Chalmers method of separating
isotopes.

Types of Nuclear Isomerism

Nuclear isomerism may be classified into types. There are
two limiting cases and a few intermediate cases lying between
the two limits. This method of classification was first adopted
by Segré and Helmholtz (1949). It may be explained with the
aid of Fig. 11.2 which represents the ground state and an
excited state of each of the two nuclei A and B. A in state 2
decays to B by β-emission with transition probability per unit
time λ_{β_2}. The probability of its transition to the ground state

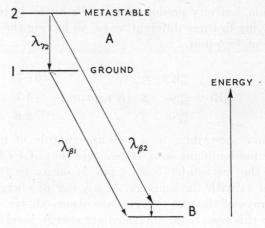

FIG. 11.2. Isomer types.

is λ_{γ_2}. Then the half-life of state 2 is

$$\tau = 0 \cdot 69/(\lambda_{\beta_2} + \lambda_{\gamma_2})$$

and the branching ratio between the two activities is

$$p = \lambda_{\beta_2}/\lambda_{\gamma_2} \tag{11.1}$$

We consider two limiting cases (Fig 11.3).

First, if $p \gg 1$, A decays to B almost entirely by β-emission.
The transition from the metastable to the ground state of A is
highly forbidden. A then behaves like two independent nuclei
each with its own characteristic β-decay rate and energy,
γ-rays possibly following the β-decay (Fig. 11.3a). Examples
of this type are given in Table 11.1.

TABLE 11.1

INDEPENDENT ISOMERS

Isomer	Type of Decay	Half-life
^{49}Ca	β^-	2·5 h.
	β^-	30 m.
^{52}Mn	β^+	6·5 d.
	β^+	21 m.
^{60}Co	β^-	5·3 y.
	β^-	10·7 m.
^{71}Ge	KC	11 d.
	$\beta^|$	40 h.
^{106}Ag	KC	8·2 d.
	β^+	24·5 h.
^{134}Co	β^-	1·7 y.
	β^-	3 h.

In the second case, if $p \ll 1$, state 2 of A decays almost
entirely by γ-radiation to state 1, which is the daughter of
state 2. This case is known as a pair of genetically related
isomers (Fig. 11.3b); it resembles that often found in the field
of natural radioactivity. Suppose that, initially, equal numbers
of nuclei are in states 1 and 2. If $\lambda_{\gamma_2} < \lambda_{\beta_1}$, we shall have two
different periods with an identical β-spectrum. For at first the
β-particles come from state 1 with decay probability λ_{β_1}.
Later, as the number of nuclei in state 1 is reduced, radioactive equilibrium is attained between the two states and the
β-decay now has a decay constant λ_{γ_2} corresponding to the
transition 2 to 1, the β-spectrum remaining unaltered. This
case is illustrated by the genetically related pair, ^{80}Br.
Examples of genetically related isomers are found in Table 11.2.

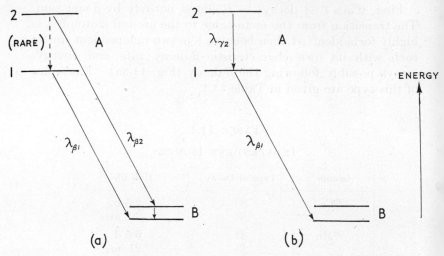

FIG. 11.3 (a) Independent isomers.   (b) Genetically related isomers.

TABLE 11.2

Isomer	Type of decay	Half-life
^{44}Sc	I.T.	2·44 d.
	β^+	3·9 h.
^{69}Zn	I.T.	13·8 h.
	β^-	57 m.
^{80}Br	I.T.	4·4 h.
	β^-	18 m.
^{81}Se	I.T.	57 m.
	β^-	19 m.
^{114}In	I.T.	48 d.
	β^-	72 s.
^{131}Te	I.T.	30 h.
	β^-	25 m.

These are the two limiting cases (Fig. 11.3 (a) and (b). We may expect however, a few intermediate cases in which $\lambda_{\gamma_2}/\lambda_{\beta_2}$ is approximately unity. Nevertheless, since these two constants both vary over a wide range of values, it is unlikely that many cases will occur in which they are of the same order

of magnitude. It should also be borne in mind that, as we saw
in the case of the isomers ^{80}Br, the isomeric transitions may be
a cascade ; between the excited and ground states of both A
and B there may occur a complicated γ-ray spectrum involving
several transitions. Moreover, in most cases the γ-rays are
internally converted, so that in place of a γ-ray spectrum there
is a line spectrum of electrons accompanied by X rays characteristic of the radioactive element.

There is a third type of isomerism, viz., that in which the
excited nuclei are isomers of stable nuclei. The decay process
is a simple transition from the metastable to the ground state
of a stable nucleus with γ-ray emission. If the γ-radiation is
converted there will be a β-particle line spectrum and characteristic X radiation. Specimens of this type are found in
Table 11.3.

TABLE 11.3

ISOMERS OF STABLE NUCLEI

Isomer	Type of Decay	Half-life
^{83}Kr*	I.T.	1·88 h.
^{87}Sr*	I.T.	2·75 h.
^{103}Rh*	I.T.	52 m.
^{107}Ag*	I.T.	44·3 s.
^{114}In*	I.T.	48·5 d.
^{197}Au*	I.T.	7·4 s.

The large majority of isomers may be classified either in this
group involving simple isomeric transition or under one of the
two limiting cases $p \gg 1$ or $p \ll 1$. More than 75 isomers have
been identified at the time of writing (1954) and more, especially
those of short life, are likely to be discovered with the aid of
new methods now being developed. The range of half-lives,
which now vary in observed cases between fractions of a second
to several years, is likely to be extended in both directions.

Theory of Isomerism

The explanation of isomeric states which has gained general
acceptance was put forward in 1936 by von Weizsäcker. He

suggested that, if a relatively small energy difference between the excited state and ground state of a nucleus was associated with a large spin difference between the nucleus in the one state and in the other, the transition would be forbidden, that is, the probability of the transition would be reduced. Thus, the nucleus in the metastable state would have a measurable lifetime. This hypothesis would gain substantial support if it were shown experimentally that spin differences of an isomer in its different energy states were considerable. Unfortunately, sufficient information on this point is still lacking. There are, however, other facts which support von Weizsäcker's hypothesis. These may be summarized in two rules stated by Mattauch :

(1) *Nuclei containing an even number of protons and of neutrons do not exist in metastable states.*

(2) *All nuclei having a spin 9/2 in the ground state have a metastable state.*

The explanation of the first rule is that these nuclei have zero spin and an energy in the ground state which is much lower than that of even the first excited state. This wide spacing of energy levels is not consistent with metastability.

The explanation of the second rule is also not far to seek. Nuclei with a spin 9/2 are of odd mass numbers and the most probable value of the spin for such nuclei is 1/2. If, therefore, the spin of the first excited state of such nuclei is 1/2, metastability is probable.

Both these explanations are based on the belief, first, that large changes in spin in isomeric transitions correspond with long half-lives, and small changes with short half-lives ; and second, that small energy changes correspond with long half-lives and large energy changes with short half-lives.

A third rule may be tentatively added to the two given above. While it is not supported by as much evidence as is desirable, no exception to it has hitherto been discovered :

(3) *No nuclei having a spin of 3/2 or 5/2 in the ground state have a metastable state.*

That the decay constant of isomeric transitions is strongly dependent on the change of spin number ΔI is brought into evidence by plotting the disintegration energies ($\log W$) of isomer

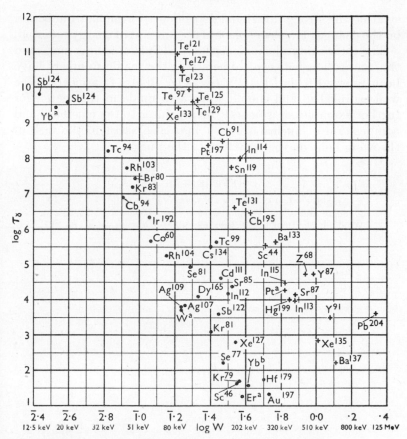

Fig. 11.4. Grouping of Isomers according to spin changes.
$\Delta I = 4\,(\bullet)$ $\Delta I = 5\,(+)$ From *Phys. Rev*, 1946, 69, 567.

against their half-lives $\log \tau$. This fact was first pointed out by Weidenbeck (1946), who, after introducing a theoretical correction to allow for internal conversion, showed convincingly that the isomers are divisible into groups according to the value of the change of spin involved. This is shown in Fig. 11.4 from which it is clear that the plotted points representing the isomers are grouped about two straight lines corresponding to spin changes $\Delta I = 4$ and $\Delta I = 5$. Other ways of graphically presenting the facts, notably that of Axel and Dancoff (1949) who introduced further corrections, are conclusive in demonstrating the strong functional dependence of the half-life period on the change of nuclear spin and the amount of energy radiated.

The interesting phenomenon of " islands of isomerism " and the connection between isomers and the magic numbers have been referred to in Chap. X (see Fig. 10.5). It appears to be well established and should serve as a guide in the search for further examples of isomers. As a pointer to the existence and composition of nuclear shells it may also assist in the task of throwing light on the structure of the nuclei.

REFERENCES

E. Amaldi *et al.*, 1935, *Ricerca Scientificia*, **61**, 581.
E. Segré and A. C. Helmholtz, 1949, *Rev. Mod. Phys.*, **21**, 2, 275.
Weidenbeck, 1946, *Phys. Rev.*, **69**, 567.

CHAPTER XII

THE ORIGIN OF THE ELEMENTS

ONE of the most remarkable facts revealed by the mass spectrograph is the constancy of the isotopic constitution of the elements. With but very few exceptions the relative abundance of the isotopes of an element found in one part of the earth's crust is identical with that found in any other part and with that found in meteorites. Astrophysical studies also indicate that the relative abundances of nuclear species are universal quantities. Moreover, the decay constants of the natural radioactive elements suggest that they all originated at the same epoch. These and other facts lend plausibility to the view that the nuclear species throughout the stellar universe had a beginning in a set of identical physical conditions at a time common to them all. It seems probable that the observed abundance distributions are to be explained by an understanding of the processes by which the elements were originally formed, for they are composed of the same elementary particles and, as we have shown, there is a significant correlation between the systematics of the nuclei and their cosmic abundance. Several theories have been formulated to account for the origin and present relative abundance of the elements and their isotopic constitution. In this Chapter we shall present some of the experimental data on which the theories are based, indicating briefly how, according to an attractive theory which has gained wide support, the facts may be explained. Finally, we shall show how the age of the elements may be estimated from the data of radioactivity.

Relative Abundance of the Elements

The incentive to speculation concerning the origin of nuclear species has come largely from the compilation of more accurate tables of their relative abundances. The early work of Goldschmidt (1938) has been supplemented by Brown (1949), who contributed data derived from the study of stellar, meteoric and cosmic abundances. This work has confirmed the remarkable constancy of the chemical and isotopic abundances throughout the universe. The abundances obtained from terrestrial measurements are, in fact, *cosmic* abundances.

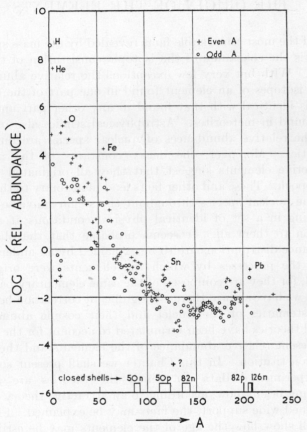

FIG. 12.1. Relative abundance of nuclear species as a function of mass numbers.

There are a few exceptions to the general rule which can easily be explained quite simply. For example, the low terrestrial abundances of hydrogen and helium, the two most plentiful elements in the stars, are due to their low densities. The difference in the abundances of radiogenic lead is easily explained in terms of its known origin. On the other hand, Unsöld has shown that the relative abundances of hydrogen and helium are the same for all stars of the main sequence. Such exceptions are unimportant in this connection.

The invariance of relative abundances of the elements throughout the stellar universe is clearly a conclusion of the greatest interest and significance. The relative abundances of nuclear species (per 10,000 atoms of silicon) *versus* mass number are shown in Fig. 12.1. Brown has stated that the abundance figures are reliable within a factor of 4, the majority within a factor of 2. With this assurance we may notice some striking features of Fig. 12.1.

The most outstanding of these is the difference between the light elements and the heavy elements. The data may indeed be represented by two straight lines, one in the region $0 < A < 100$ representing a rough exponential decrease in relative abundance, the other in the region $100 < A < 240$ showing a relative abundance which is approximately constant. The abundances of the light elements vary irregularly, those of the heavy elements do not.

The most striking irregularity is the peak in the neighbourhood of Fe where the abundance is above the normal in this region by a factor of 10^4. Other peaks, showing a deviation from the general trend, are found in the region of the magic number nuclides, 50 or 82 protons, or 50, 82, 126 neutrons. The peak at lead ($Z = 82$, $N = 126$) is conspicuous. The special stability of these nuclides is reflected in the abundance data (Table 5.7, p. 90).

The superior abundance of nuclides of even A over those of odd A, a consequence of their superior stability, is also clearly shown in Fig. 12.1. A similar differentiation is seen in a plot of relative abundances *versus* atomic number. Elements of even Z are almost invariably more abundant than those of odd Z.

These are the main facts apparent from Fig. 1. There is another fact of great importance which also distinguishes the light from the heavy elements of even Z-values. A comparison of the abundance of the lightest isotope of a given element with that of the heaviest shows that for light elements ($Z < 34$) the lightest isotope is abundant and the heaviest rare. For heavy elements $(Z \geqslant 34)$ the opposite holds. The first example is selenium $(Z = 34)$. The abundance of $^{74}_{34}$Se is 0·84%, whereas that of $^{82}_{34}$Se is 9·19%. For all heavier elements $(Z > 34)$, with five exceptions (four of which have closed shells), the heaviest isotope is never rare, whereas the abundance of the lightest isotope never exceeds 1·4%. The difference in isotope abundance distributions which distinguishes the light from the heavy elements is illustrated in Fig. 12.2, in which the relative abundance of typical $(Z$ even) isotopes are shown, one for $Z < 34$ and one for $Z > 34$. This important result of mass spectra measurements is a starting point of every hypothesis of the origin of the heavier elements which has hitherto been put forward.

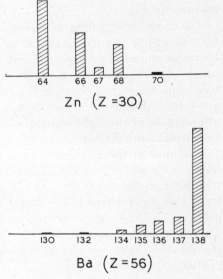

Another rule which bears on the problem of the origin of the elements has reference to the relative abundance of isobars. Out of 51 examples of stable isobars, in 44 cases the isobar of lower Z is the more abundant. We shall refer to this later.

One further observation

FIG. 12.2. Isotope abundance of two elements $(Z < 34$ and $Z > 34)$.

is relevant. It has been shown that there is a correlation between the neutron-capture cross sections (σ) and mass number. In fact, there is a rough linear inverse correlation between $\log \sigma$ and $\log$ (abundance). Whereas the relative abundances decrease exponentially with increasing atomic mass to $A \simeq 100$ and remain constant for $A > 100$, the neutron-capture cross sections increase exponentially to $A \simeq 100$ and thereafter remain about constant.

In formulating an hypothesis to account for the formation

of the elements the facts set out above must be considered in conjunction with convergent lines of evidence relating to the age of the elements. We shall see that there is reason to believe that all radioactive nuclei found in nature were formed several thousand million years ago. The estimates of the age of the earth, of meteorites and of the stellar universe all point to the same epoch.

According to geological measurements the earth's age is between 3×10^9 and 4×10^9 years. One method of estimation depends on the measurements of the helium content of uranium ores. It has been calculated that a gram of uranium produces in a single half-life 376 c.c. of helium at normal temperature and pressure. Although the gas would tend to escape from the uranium ore, making an estimate of its age unreliable, measurement of the amount of helium still retained would give a minimum value of the age of the ore. Other methods have been used. The ultimate disintegration product of the uranium series is stable lead and the determination of the uranium/lead ratio has been applied to the estimation of the age of the ore containing these elements.

The age of meteorites has also been deduced from their helium content, but the method is not so trustworthy. As was pointed out by Huntley (1948), the bombardment of a meteorite by cosmic rays for periods of the order of hundreds of millions of years would cause nuclear disintegrations which, by augmenting the quantity of helium produced by an unknown amount, would vitiate the conclusions.

The shift to the red in the spectra of distant galaxies has led to the belief that the universe is rapidly expanding. Calculations based on the rate of expansion point to an epoch when, the expansion not having yet begun, the matter from which the galaxies originated was in a state of high density. This epoch is computed to be about 2×10^9 years ago. The array of evidence thus tends to support the conclusion that the formation of the elements took place at the time when the condensed primeval mass of undifferentiated matter began to expand. It has led to a theory which, while it may seem fantastic, nevertheless accounts in a qualitative way for many of the facts discussed in the foregoing pages.

182   NUCLEAR SPECIES

Neutron-Capture Theory

The theory supposes that at the beginning of the cosmic expansion, which, according to von Weizsäcker, was of explosive violence, there existed nothing but elementary particles (neutrons predominating) and radiation at a high temperature. The density was high but not high enough to prevent the decay of neutrons into protons. In the early stages the formation of light nuclei would be hindered by the high temperatures and by photo-disintegration processes. Later, when the primeval mass had cooled by expansion, deuterons were formed in accordance with the reaction $^1H(n, \gamma)^2D$. From these the heavier nuclei were built up by the successive capture of neutrons. A startling feature of the theory is that this building-up process must have been completed in a very short period of time, of the order of a few neutron lifetimes, measurable in minutes (Gamow and Critchfield, 1949). This is because, first, the initial high concentration of neutrons would be rapidly reduced by neutron β-decay and by capture, and, second, the reaction rates would diminish as a consequence of the dilution of matter produced by expansion. That the density of the expanding primeval mass required for the formation of the nuclear species would be critical, enduring therefore for a short period only, may be understood in a qualitative way by noting that a very low density would yield only protons whereas a very high density would produce the neutron-rich heavy nuclei in too great an abundance.

Another important process which would operate contemporaneously with neutron capture is the decay by negatron emission of the too neutron-rich nuclei. The emissions of β-particles from successive isobars would continue until a stable isobar was reached.

Summarizing, the neutron-capture theory supposes that the elements were formed in an interval of time, measured in minutes, at the pre-stellar epoch when the expansion of the primary substance, comprising all matter in the form of a dense conglomeration of neutrons at high temperature, was beginning ; that the formation process was, essentially, successive neutron capture with intervening β-decay ; and that the building-up was terminated suddenly as the dilution by expansion of the dense primeval mass passed a critical density phase.

The theory is not without its difficulties but it does start from an assumption for which the evidence is strong, viz., that there was " in the beginning " a period of great neutron excess. Without this excess it is hard to see how the heavy nuclei came into existence at all. Moreover, it accounts satisfactorily for the observation that the heavy isotopes of the heavy elements of higher isotopic number are more abundant than the light isotopes. It explains also the fact that of a pair of isobars the one of the lower Z-value is generally the more abundant. The theory supposes that a too neutron-rich nucleus, by β-decay, passed through the successive isobar stages until a point of stability in the Heisenberg valley was reached. Thus, the stable isobar $_{Z}^{4}X$ would receive contributions from the decay of the isobars $_{Z-1}^{4}X$, $_{Z-2}^{4}X$ ... , all of which were too rich in neutrons for stability. The other isobar of higher Z-value, $_{Z+2}^{4}X$, would receive no such contributions and would consequently have a smaller relative abundance. If these arguments are valid it would appear that the final form of the abundance distributions of the isotopes was determined by β-decay processes.

Further support for the theory that the elements originated in a neutron-capture process is the fact already noted of the inverse correlation between capture cross-section and relative abundance. With this is associated the observations (i) that the closed shell nuclei, which have relatively small neutron-capture cross-sections, have relatively high abundance and (ii) that even-A nuclei are more abundant than odd-A nuclei.

The neutron-capture theory does not explain the peak in the abundance curve in the vicinity of iron. Neither has any other theory accounted for this anomaly. The theory also fails to take into account the non-existence of nuclei of atomic masses 5 and 8. How these gaps were bridged and a formation chain constructed through the lightest elements is not clear. While alternative theories have been put forward to explain the origin of the elements—an excellent review article of these has been written by Alpher and Herman (1950)—the neutron-capture theory probably gives rise to fewer difficulties than the others and it has the merit that, while demanding a rather too well defined cosmological model as a background, it fits in with the astrophysicists' ideas of the origin and present constitution of an expanding universe.

The Age of the Elements

It is the existence of the natural, unstable nuclear species, slowly decaying through geological ages, which compels the belief that these nuclides at least must have had their origin at a definite epoch. The facts of radioactive decay also throw light on the problem of the age of the earth. It is possible, with the aid of a knowledge of the half-life periods of the naturally radioactive species, assuming that their rate of decay has remained constant from the beginning, to fix their age within certain upper and lower limits.

The absence of neptunium and plutonium from the earth's crust points to a lower limit to the earth's age. It is true that a trace of ^{239}Pu (about 1 atom of ^{239}Pu in 10^{14} atoms of natural uranium) has been found in natural uranium, but this is assumed to have been produced by neutrons arising from the spontaneous fission of uranium. If we suppose that the original abundances of, say, neptunium and uranium were about equal and that the relative abundance today is less than $1 : 10^{15}$, we may establish a lower limit to the age of the earth.

Let n_1, n_2 be the original numbers of atoms of uranium and neptunium respectively in a given mass of primeval matter, and let N_1, N_2 be the number of atoms found today in the same mass.

Then

$$N_1 = n_1 e^{-\lambda_1 t} \quad \text{and} \quad N_2 = n_2 e^{-\lambda_2 t}$$

where λ_1 and λ_2 are the decay constants of uranium and neptunium respectively and t is the period of decay. Hence

$$\frac{N_1}{N_2} \cdot \frac{n_2}{n_1} = e^{(\lambda_2 - \lambda_1)t}. \tag{12.1}$$

If τ_1 and τ_2 are the half-life periods of the elements,

$$\ln\left(\frac{N_1}{N_2} \cdot \frac{n_2}{n_1}\right) = (\lambda_2 - \lambda_1)t$$

so that

$$2\cdot303\left\{\log\left(N_1/N_2\right)+\log\left(n_2/n_1\right)\right\}=\left(\frac{1}{\tau_2}-\frac{1}{\tau_1}\right)t. \qquad (12.2)$$

Now the half-life of ^{238}U (τ_1) is $4\cdot51\times10^9$ years while that of neptunium is $2\cdot25\times10^6$ years (Table 12.1), so that $1/\tau_1$ may be neglected in comparison with $1/\tau_2$. We have assumed that N_1/N_2 is not less than 10^{15} and that n_1/n_2 is about unity.

Eq. (12.2) accordingly becomes

$$2\cdot303\left(\log 10^{15}+\log 1\right)=t/\tau_2$$

so that $\qquad\qquad t=34\cdot5\,\tau_2$

Thus the age of the earth must exceed about 35 half-lives of neptunium, or eighty million years. A lower value of this limit would require that a greater concentration than 1 atom Np to 10^{15} atoms ^{238}U should be found in the earth's crust. Actually, the concentration is very much less than this.

TABLE 12.1

Isotope	Relative Isotopic Abundance %	Activity	Half-life (10^9 years)
^{39}K	93·38	None	
^{40}K	0·012	β	0·24
^{41}K	6·61	None	
^{147}Sm	15·07	None	
^{148}Sm	11·27	α	140
^{149}Sm	13·84	None	
^{85}Rb	72·8	None	
^{87}Rb	27·2	β	63
^{232}Th	100·0	α	13·9
^{235}U	0·719	α	0·707
^{238}U	99·274	α	4·51
^{237}Np		α	0·00225

It may be objected that our assumption of the initial quantitative equivalence of the two elements $(n_1=n_2)$ is without observational support. That is true, but Eq. (12.2) shows that the value of t is not very sensitive to the value of n_2/n_1, since t is certainly a long enough period to make n_2/n_1 negligible in comparison with N_1/N_2. We may accordingly take it that the age of the earth exceeds 80×10^6 years. Let us now attempt to find an upper limit to the age of certain radioactive elements and hence to the age of the earth.

We note that at the present time the relative abundances of thorium (232) and of neighbouring elements such as stable bismuth are about equal, that is, using our previous notation, $N_1 \simeq N_2$. It follows that at the epoch when the elements were formed there was some excess of thorium over bismuth. If we now assume that this excess was small, Eq. 12.2 becomes

$$2 \cdot 303 \log(1+) = t/\tau$$

so that t is a fraction of the half-life of ^{232}Th, which is $13 \cdot 9 \times 10^9$ years. Thus, if our basic assumption is granted, we can make a very crude estimate : it would appear that the age of the earth cannot be less than one hundred million years nor greater than several thousand million years.

Instead of assuming that the relative abundances of the *elements* were approximately equal when they were formed, we might suppose that a naturally radioactive *isotope* was originally approximately as abundant as one of its neighbours in the isotope family and hence calculate the age of the element in terms of the half-life of the active isotope. Applying this to ^{39}K and ^{40}K we find from Table 12.1 that $N_1/N_2 = 93380/12$ so that, from Eq. (12.2)

$$2 \cdot 303 (\log 7782 + \log 1) = \left(\frac{1}{\tau_2} - \frac{1}{\tau_1}\right) t$$

Since ^{39}K is stable, $1/\tau_1$, is zero and

$$t = 9 \text{ half-lives of } {}^{40}\text{K}$$

This is about $2 \cdot 2 \times 10^9$ years. If we had used the figures for the relative abundance of ^{40}K and ^{41}K (Table 12.1), we should have obtained $6 \cdot 3$ half-lives or $1 \cdot 5 \times 10^9$ years.

A similar calculation for the isotopes ^{235}U and ^{238}U yields $4 \cdot 1 \times 10^9$ years as the value of t.

If this figure of several thousand million years may be taken as the right order of value of the age of these radioactive elements—and it is in harmony with other independent methods of estimation—the assumption of the primeval equality of isotopic abundance cannot be valid for those radioactive isotopes, such as ^{87}Rb and ^{148}Sm, the half-lives of which are ten times and a hundred times the period during which they have existed.

It is hardly surprising in view of the order of accuracy of the basic data at our disposal, that the results of the various methods of calculating the age of the elements are not in precise agreement. It is rather a cause for surprise and congratulation that results of the same order of magnitude are obtained from the widely different methods of geology, astrophysics and nuclear physics. It is remarkable that such studies of nuclear species and of the systematics of the nuclei as are outlined in these pages are able to shed light on the problem of the origin and the age of the universe as the astronomer describes it today.

REFERENCES

R. A. Alpher and R. C. Herman, 1950, *Rev. Mod. Phys.*, **22**, (2), 153.

H. Brown, 1949, *Rev. Mod. Phys.*, **21**, 625.

Gamow and Critchfield, 1949, *Atomic Nucleus and Nuclear Energy-Sources*, p. 309.

V. M. Goldschmidt, 1938, *Verteilungsgesetze der Elemente*.

H. E. Huntley, 1948, *Nature*, **161**, 4088, 356.

(a) Values of Natural Constants

Velocity of light	c	$(2 \cdot 99776 \pm 0 \cdot 00004) \times 10^{10}$ cm. sec.$^{-1}$.
Planck's constant	h	$(6 \cdot 623 \pm 0 \cdot 001) \times 10^{-27}$ erg.-sec.
Charge of electron	e	$(4 \cdot 8024 \pm 0 \cdot 0005) \times 10^{-10}$ esu.
Mass of electron	m_0	$(9 \cdot 1055 \pm 0 \cdot 0012) \times 10^{-28}$ gm.
Mass of proton	M_p	$(1 \cdot 6723 \pm 0 \cdot 0001) \times 10^{-24}$ gm.
		$(1 \cdot 007582 \pm 0 \cdot 000004)$ amu.
Mass of neutron	M_n	$(1 \cdot 6747 \pm 0 \cdot 00002) \times 10^{-24}$ gm.
		$(1 \cdot 008939 \pm 0 \cdot 000007)$ amu.

(b) Conversion Factors

	Grams	Mass Units	Ergs	MeV
1 gram =	1	$6 \cdot 02 \times 10^{23}$	$9 \cdot 00 \times 10^{20}$	$5 \cdot 62 \times 10^{26}$
1 mass unit =	$1 \cdot 66 \times 10^{-24}$	1	$1 \cdot 49 \times 10^{-3}$	931
1 erg =	$1 \cdot 11 \times 10^{-21}$	671	1	$6 \cdot 24 \times 10^{5}$
1 MeV =	$1 \cdot 78 \times 10^{-27}$	$1 \cdot 07 \times 10^{-3}$	$1 \cdot 60 \times 10^{-6}$	1

Coulomb Energy of Nucleus ^AX

To calculate the total electrostatic energy of a nucleus with Z protons, consider the mutual energy of a pair of protons. Assuming that their charge (e) is spread uniformly through the nucleus, a sphere of radius r, the charge density is $3e/4\pi r^3$, so that the quantity of electricity contained in a thin shell of radius r_1 and thickness dr_1 is $3er_1^2\,dr_1/r^3$.

The mutual energy between this and a second elementary shell of radius $r_2\,(r_2 > r_1)$ corresponding to the second proton is

$$\frac{3er_1^2\,dr_1}{r^3} \cdot \frac{3er_2^2\,dr_2}{r^3} \cdot \frac{1}{r_2} = \frac{9e^2}{r^6}\, r_1^2 r_2\, dr_1\, dr_2.$$

Thus the total energy due to the portion of the charge derived from the first proton which lies within the shell of radius r_2 is

$$\frac{9e^2}{r^6} \cdot r_2\, dr_2 \int_0^{r_2} r_1^2\, dr_1 = \frac{3e^2 r_2^4\, dr_2}{r^6}.$$

This is now to be integrated with respect to r_2 and the result doubled

$$\frac{6e^2}{r^6} \int_0^r r_2^4\, dr_2 = \frac{6e^2}{5r}.$$

For a nucleus containing Z protons, since each proton repels every other proton, this result must be multiplied by $Z(Z-1)/2$. Hence the total Coulomb energy is

$$E_e = 3e^2 Z(Z-1)/5r.$$

If Z is large this is approximately $3e^2 Z^2/5r$.
The value of a_3 in Eq. (9.5) on p. 143 is obtained as follows :
Since $r = 1\cdot5 \times 10^{-13} A^{\frac{1}{3}}$ cm., approximately,

$$E_c = a_3 Z^2/A^{\frac{1}{3}} = 3e^2 Z^2/(5 \times 1\cdot5 \times 10^{-13})A^{\frac{1}{3}}$$

$$\text{i.e.,} \quad a_3 = 3e^2/7\cdot5 \times 10^{-13} \text{ ergs.}$$

Using values given in Appendix I,

$$a_3 = 0\cdot000627 \text{ amu.}$$

ALPHABETICAL LIST OF THE ELEMENTS

Element	Symbol	Atomic Number Z	Element	Symbol	Atomic Number Z
Aluminum	Al	13	Molybdenum	Mo	42
Americium	Am	95	Neodymium	Nd	60
Antimony	Sb	51	Neon	Ne	10
Argon	A	18	Neptunium	Np	93
Arsenic	As	33	Nickel	Ni	28
Astatine	At	85	Nitrogen	N	7
Barium	Ba	56	Osmium	Os	76
Beryllium	Be	4	Oxygen	O	8
Bismuth	Bi	83	Palladium	Pd	46
Boron	B	5	Phosphorus	P	15
Bromine	Br	35	Platinum	Pt	78
Cadmium	Cd	48	Plutonium	Pu	94
Calcium	Ca	20	Potassium	K	19
Carbon	C	6	Praseodymium	Pr	59
Cerium	Ce	58	Promethium	Pm	61
Cesium	Cs	55	Protactinium	Pa	91
Chlorine	Cl	17	Radium	Ra	88
Chromium	Cr	24	Radon	Rn	86
Cobalt	Co	27	Rhenium	Re	75
Columbium	Cb	41	Rhodium	Rh	45
Copper	Cu	29	Rubidium	Rb	37
Curium	Cm	96	Ruthenium	Ru	44
Dysprosium	Dy	66	Samarium	Sm	62
Erbium	Er	68	Scandium	Sc	21
Europium	Eu	63	Selenium	Se	34
Fluorine	F	9	Silicon	Si	14
Francium	Fr	87	Silver	Ag	47
Gadolinium	Gd	64	Sodium	Na	11
Gallium	Ga	31	Strontium	Sr	38
Germanium	Ge	32	Sulpher	S	16
Gold	Au	79	Tantalum	Ta	73
Hafnium	Hf	72	Technetium	Tc	43
Helium	He	2	Tellurium	Te	52
Holmium	Ho	67	Terbium	Tb	65
Hydrogen	H	1	Thallium	Tl	81
Indium	In	49	Thorium	Th	90
Iodine	I	53	Thulium	Tm	69
Iridium	Ir	77	Tin	Sn	50
Iron	Fe	26	Titanium	Ti	22
Krypton	Kr	36	Tungsten	W	74
Lanthanum	La	57	Uranium	U	92
Lead	Pb	82	Vanadium	V	23
Lithium	Li	3	Xenon	Xe	54
Lutetium	Lu	71	Ytterbium	Yb	70
Magnesium	Mg	12	Yttrium	Y	39
Manganese	Mn	25	Zinc	Zn	30
Mercury	Hg	80	Zirconium	Zr	40

INDEX OF AUTHORS

INDEX OF SUBJECTS

PRINTED IN GREAT BRITAIN
BY ROBERT MACLEHOSE AND CO. LTD
THE UNIVERSITY PRESS, GLASGOW